KINGFISHER COLORING BOOK

CRYSTAL
COLORING BOOKS

ISBN-13: 978-1987485127
ISBN-10: 1987485122

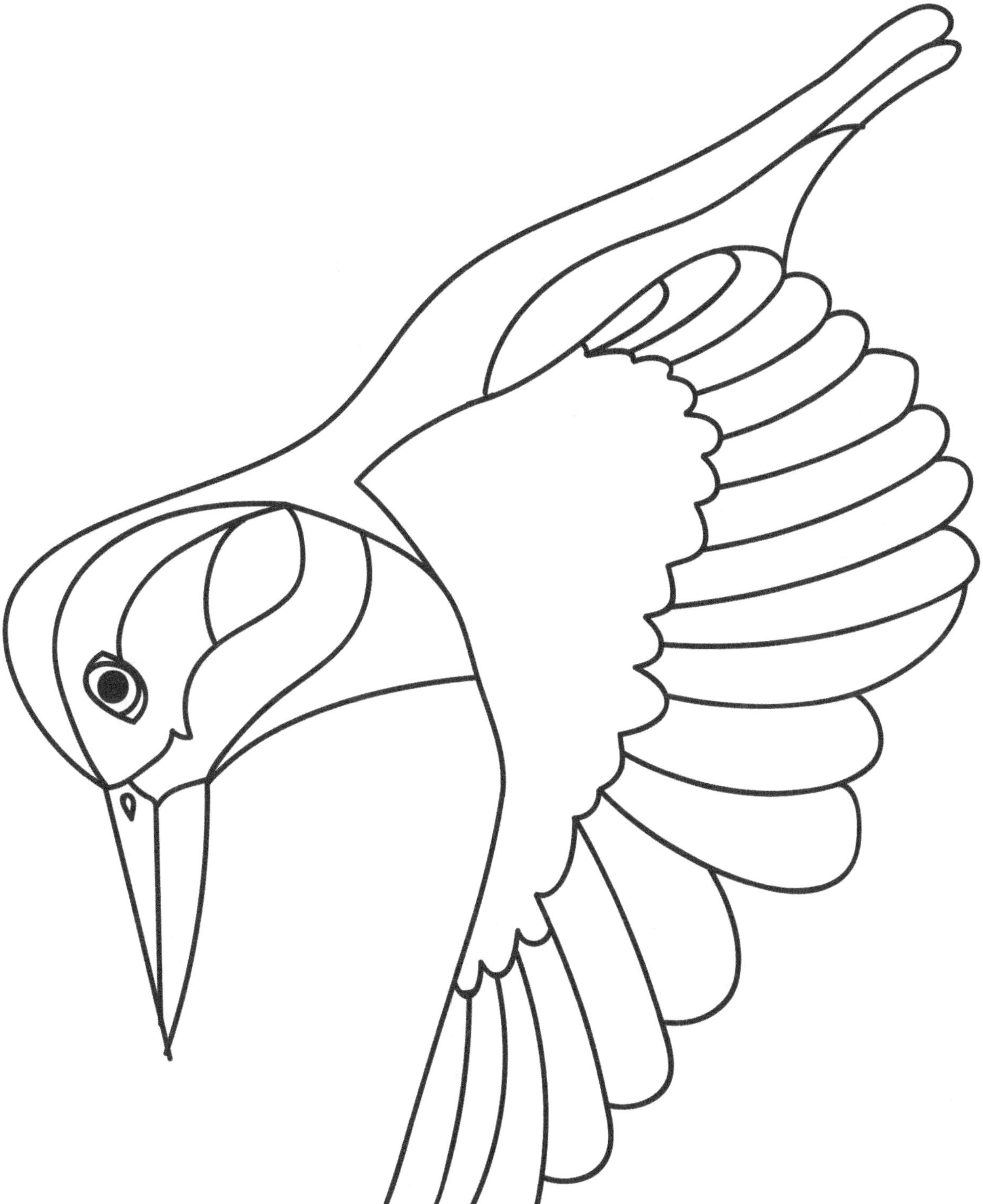

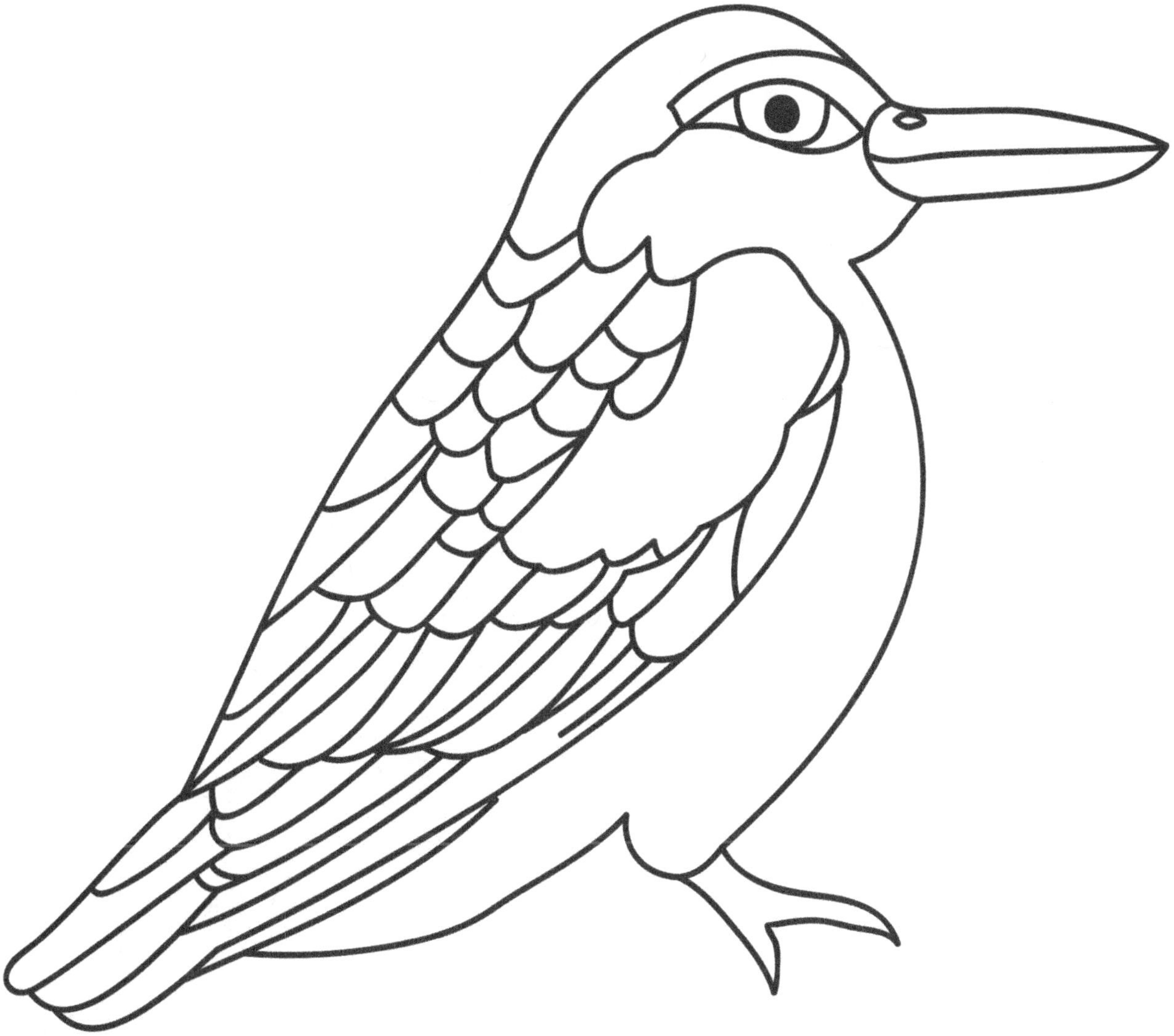

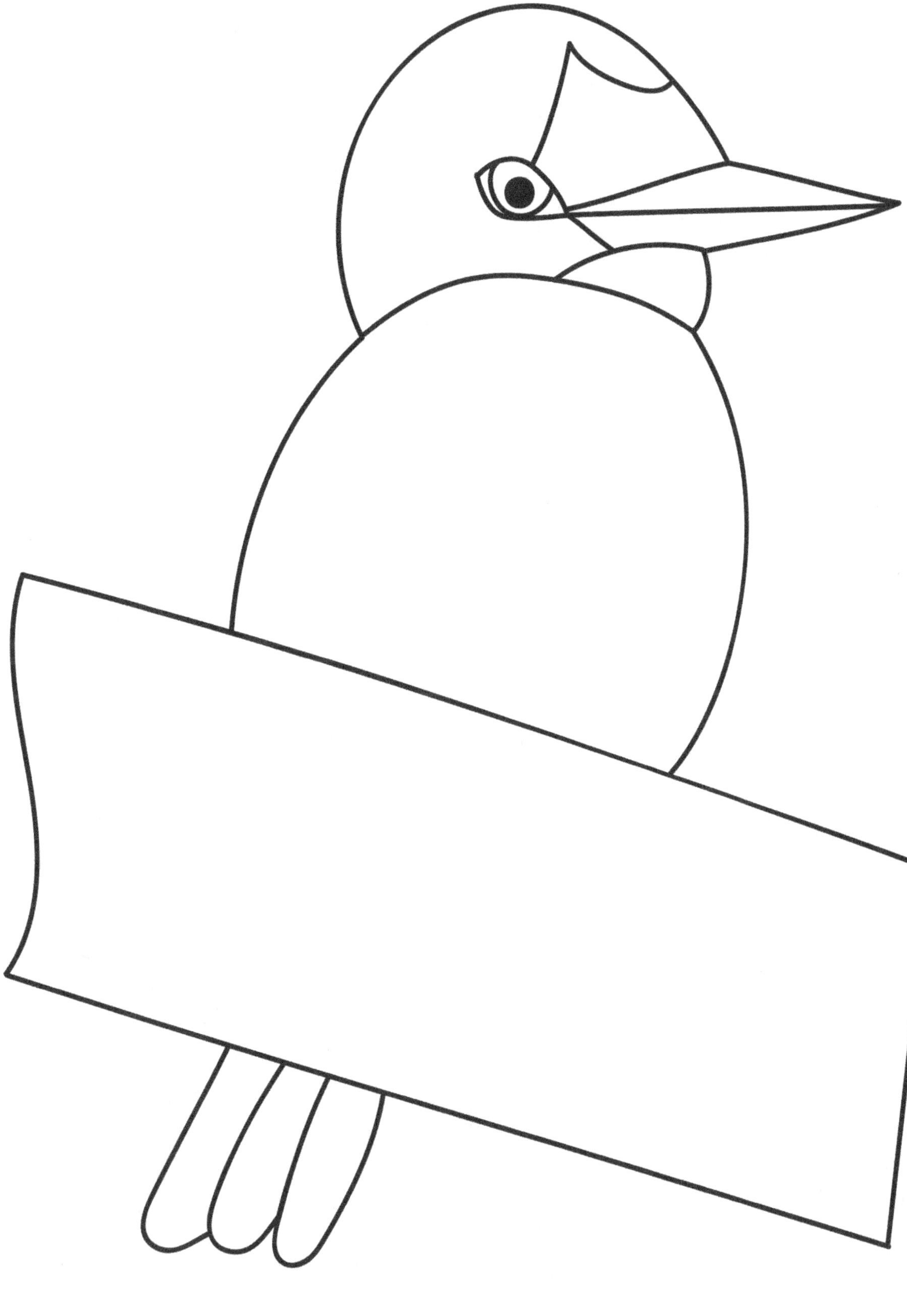

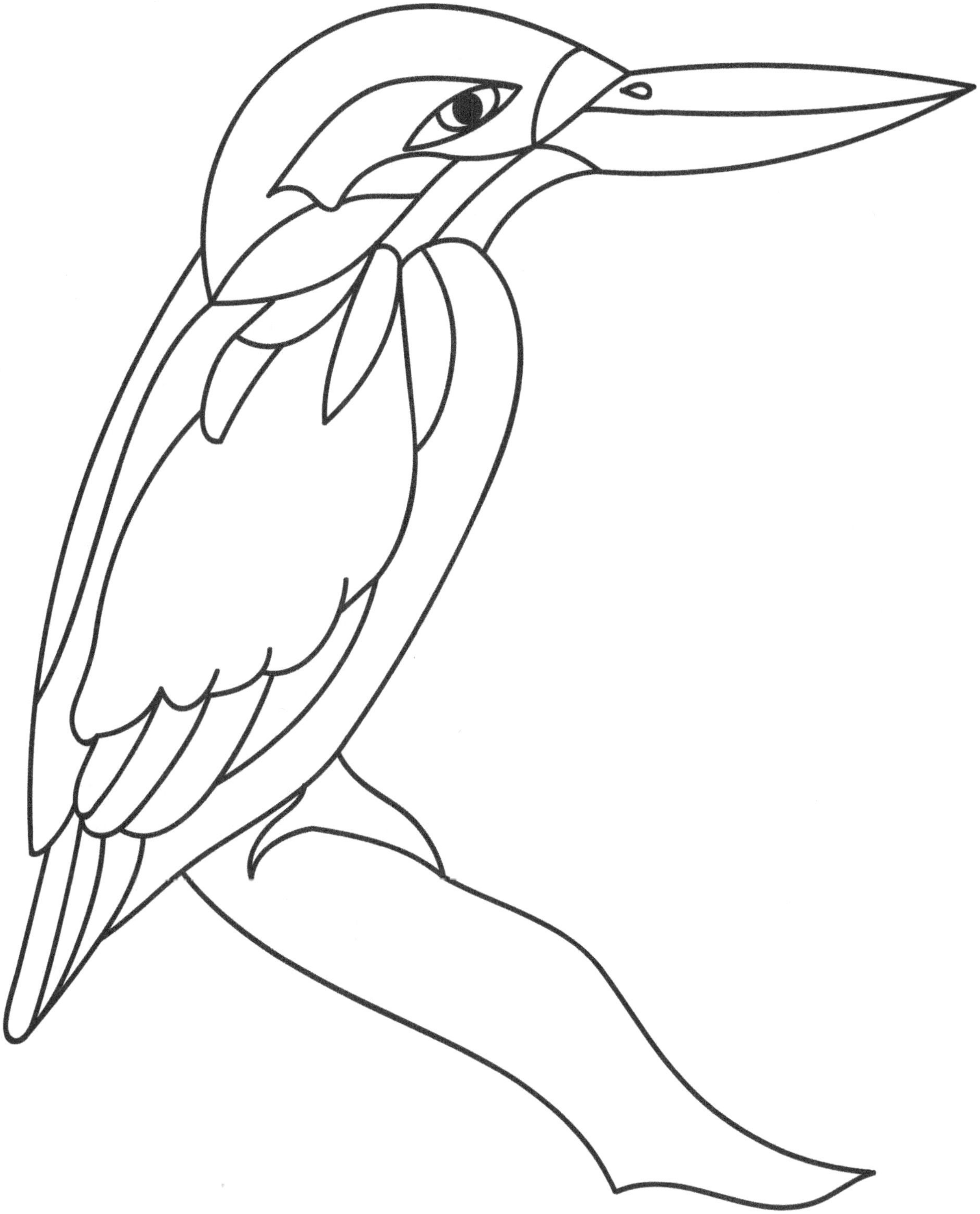

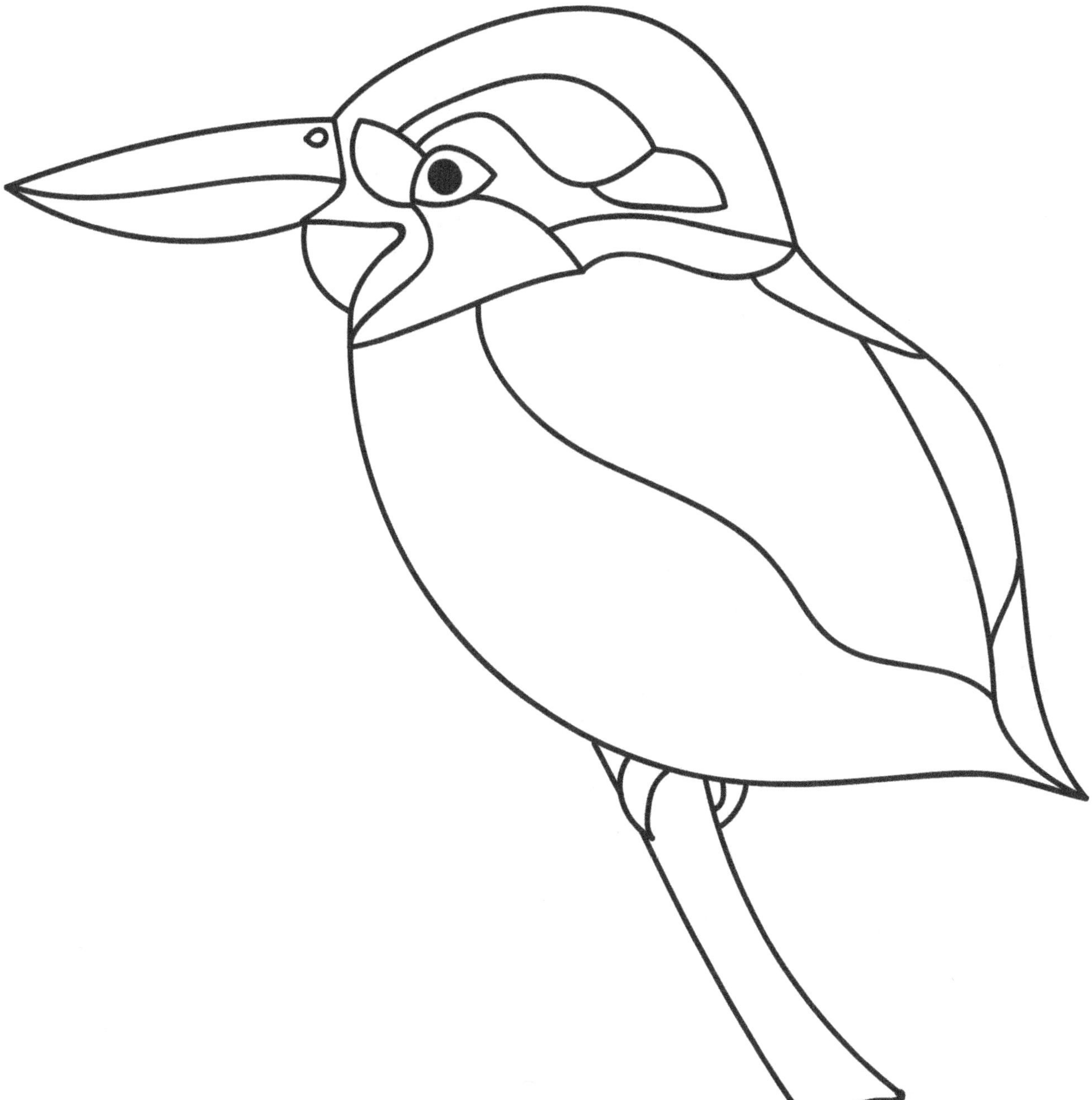

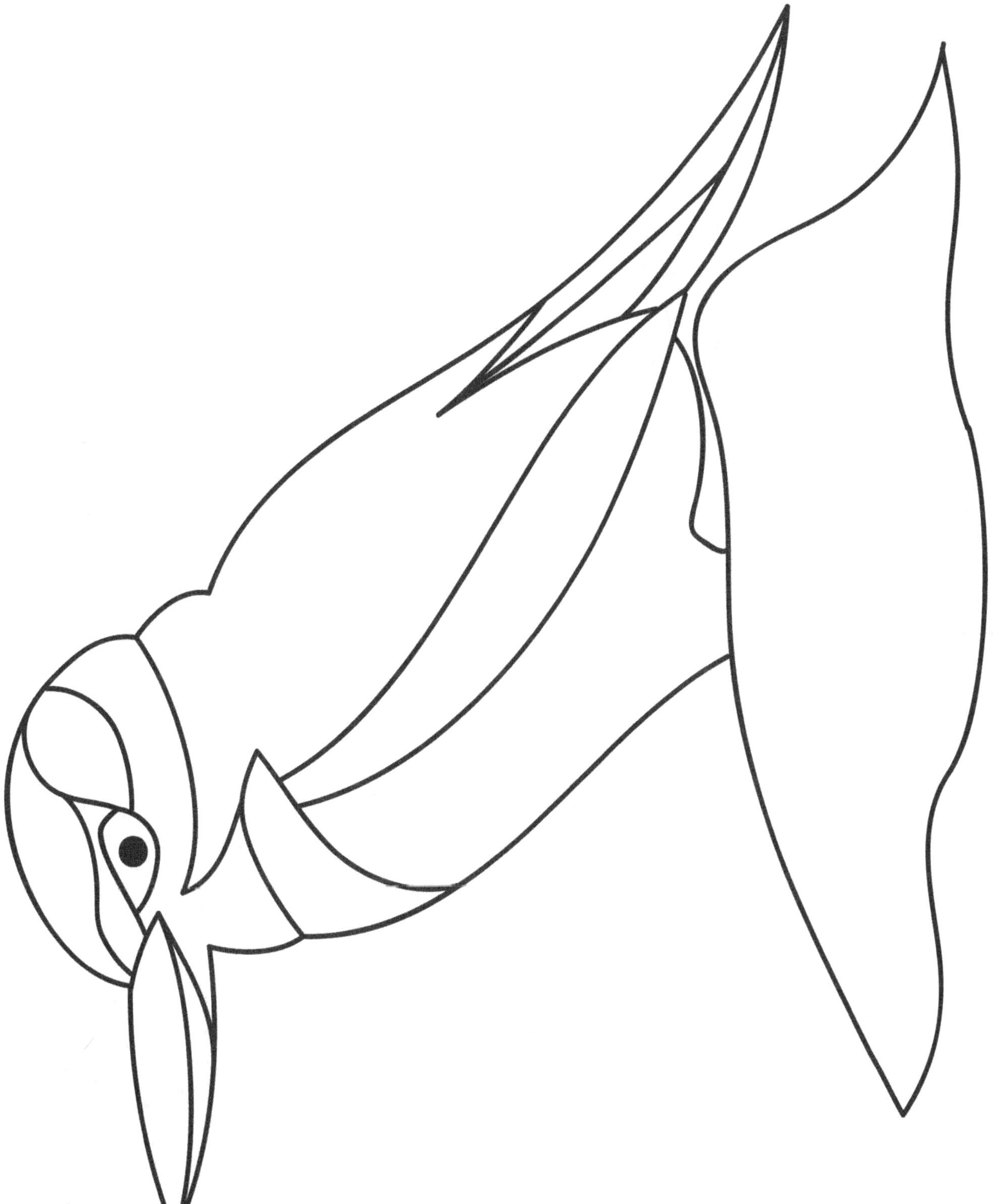

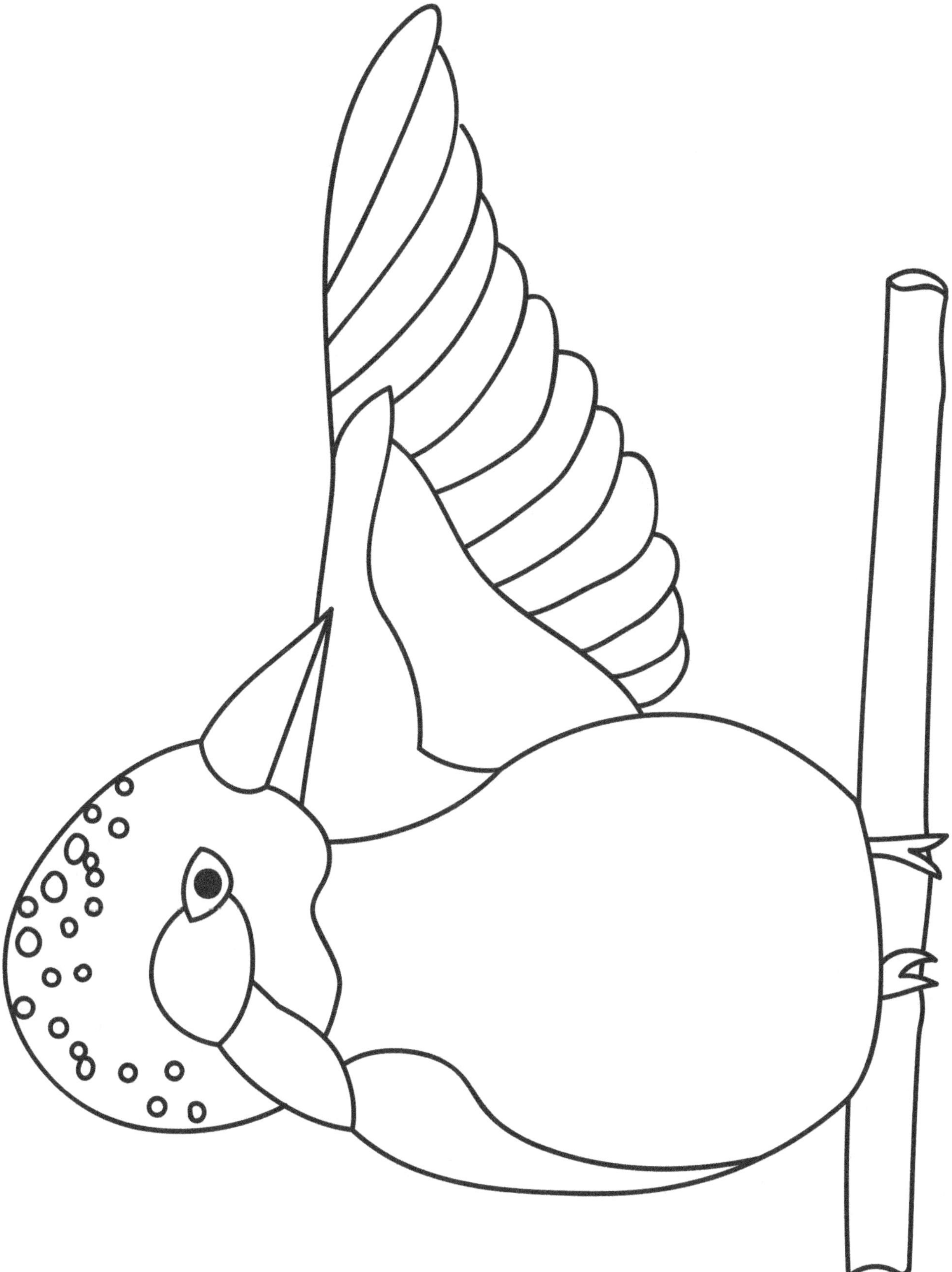

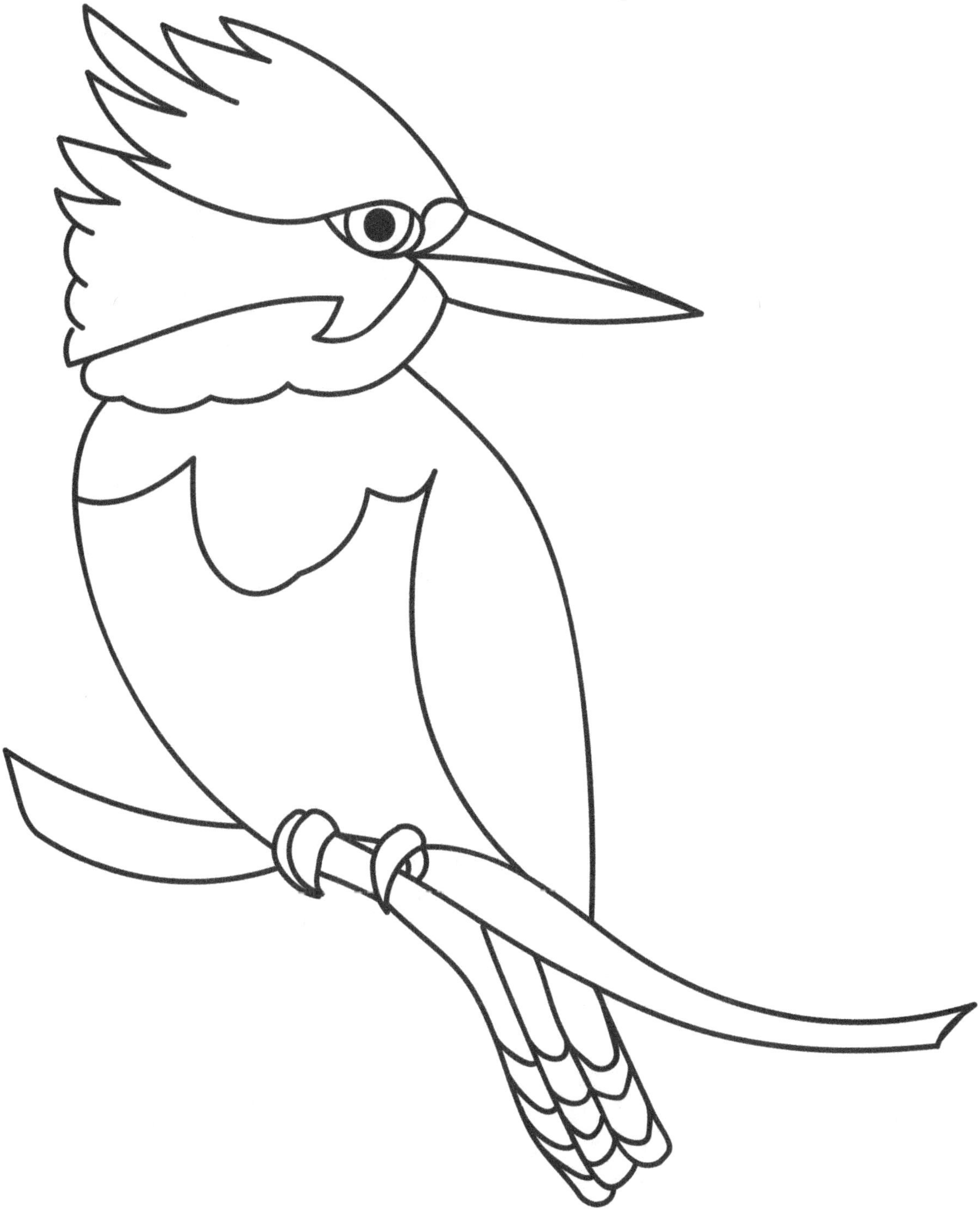

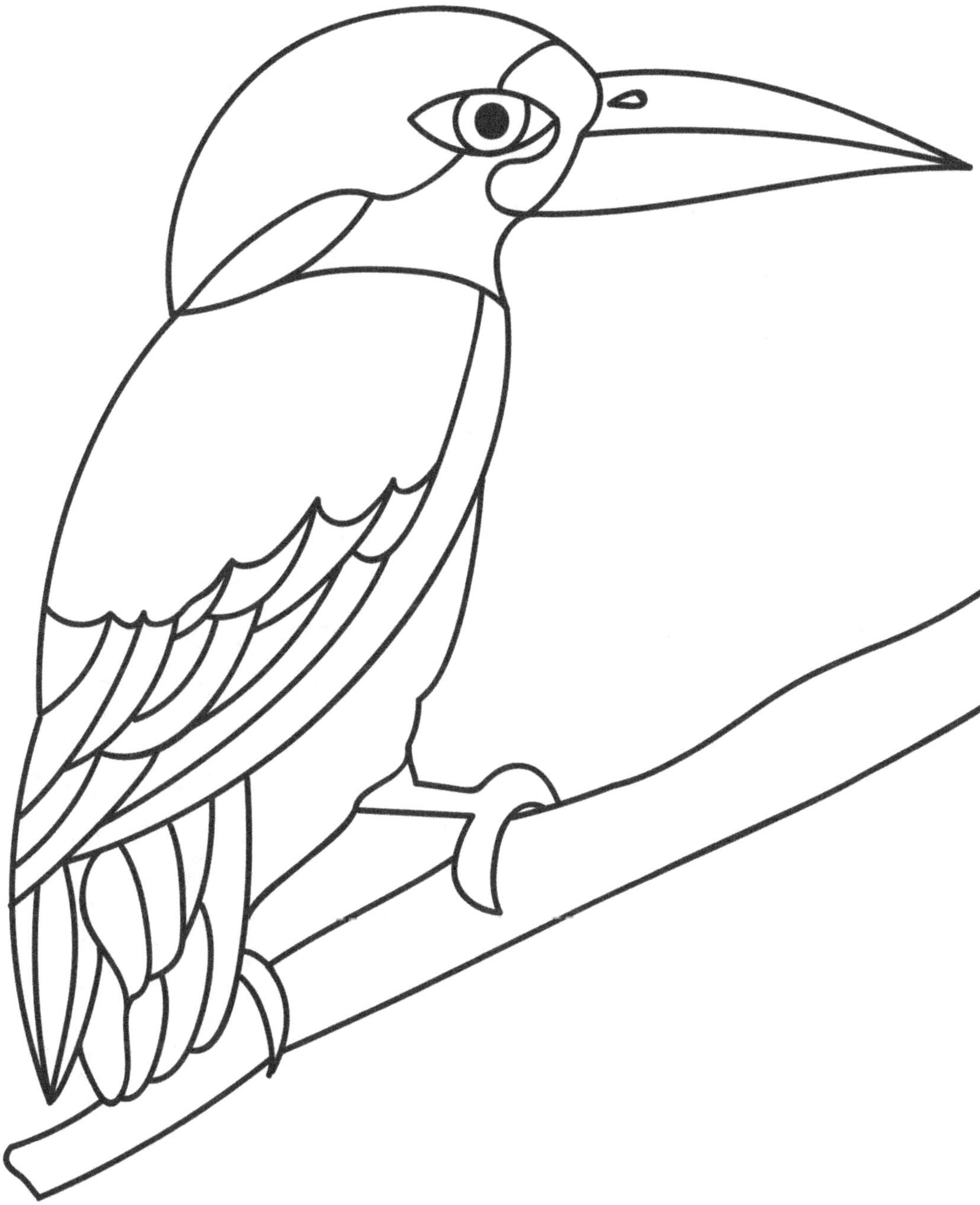

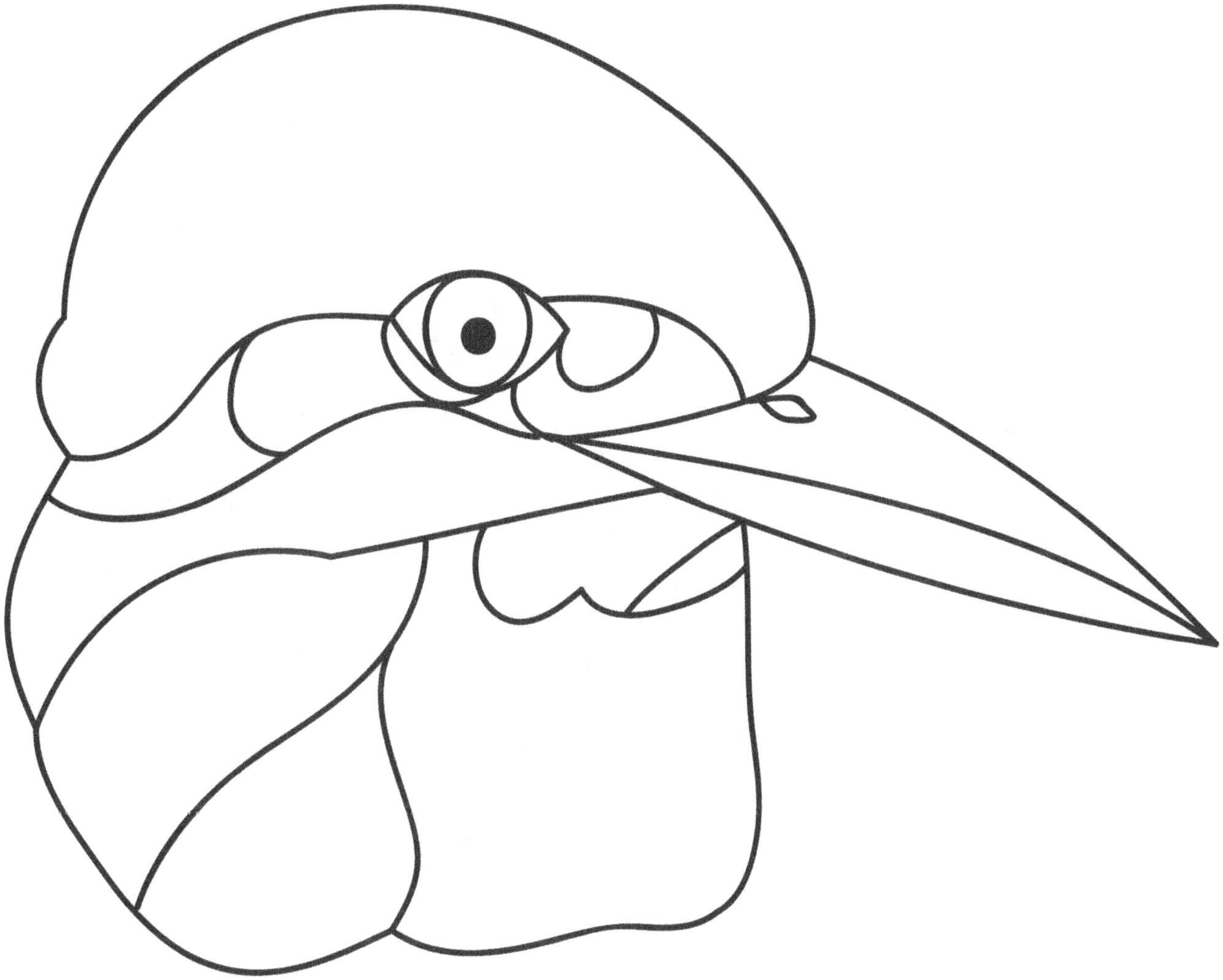

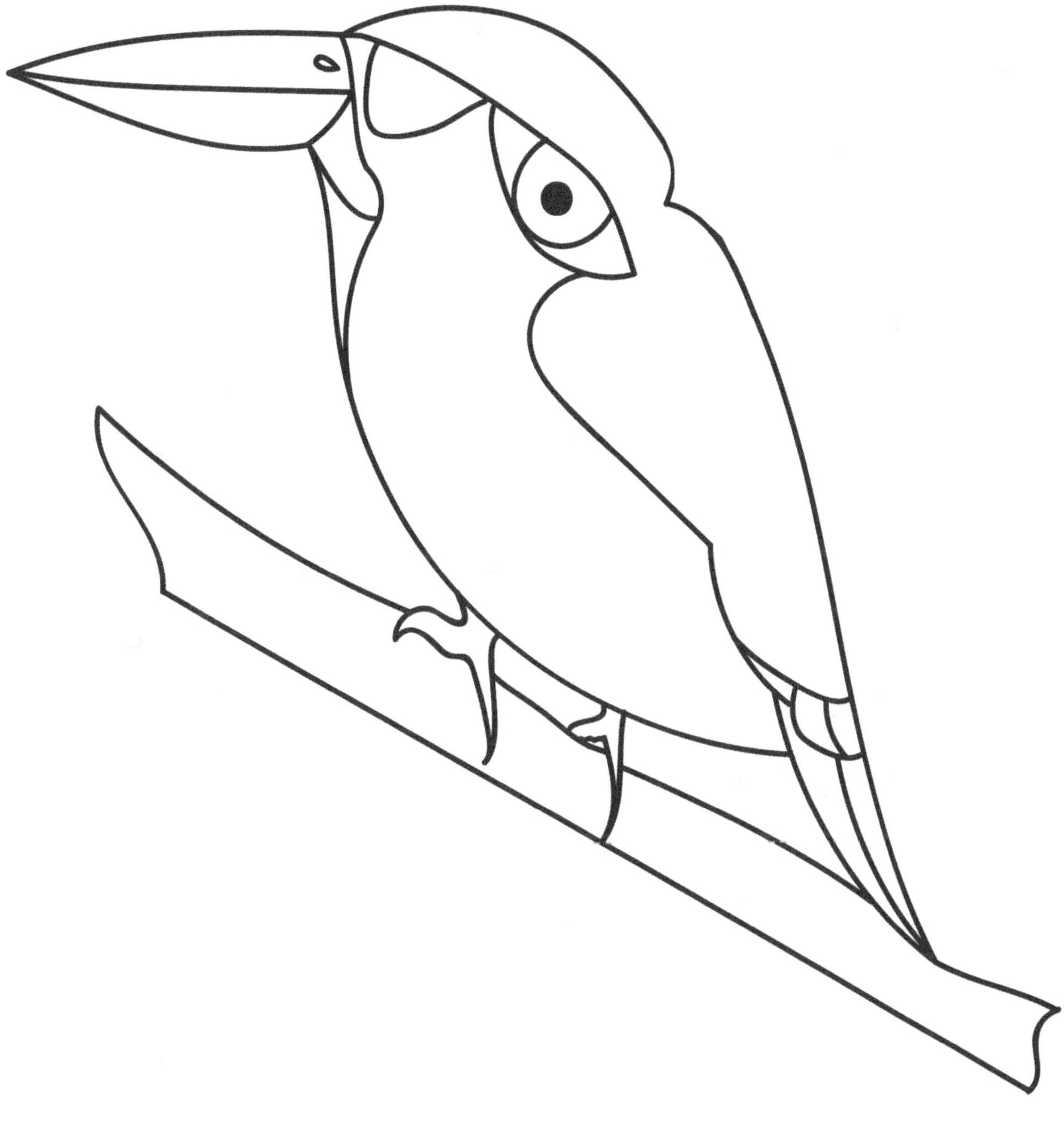

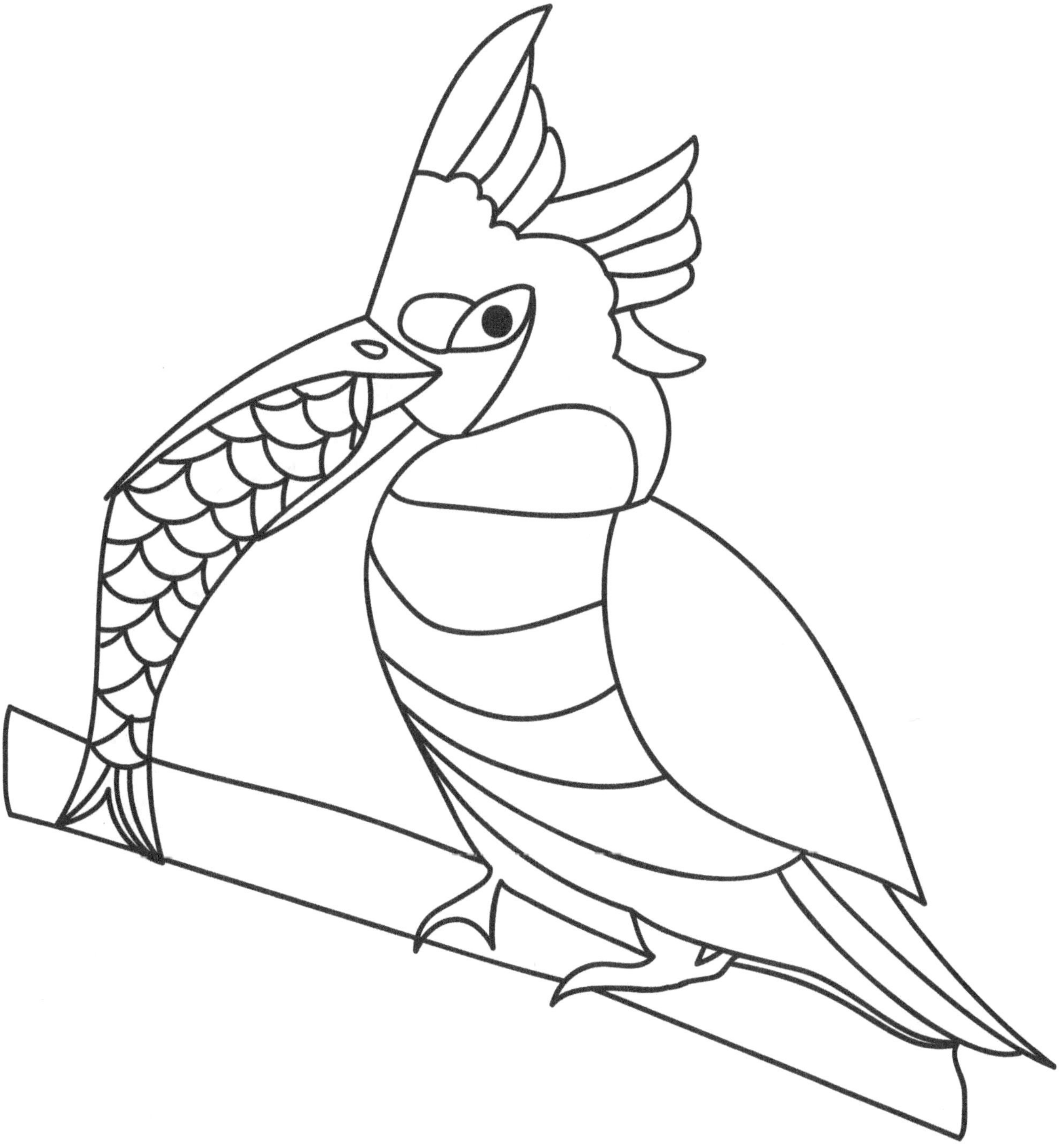

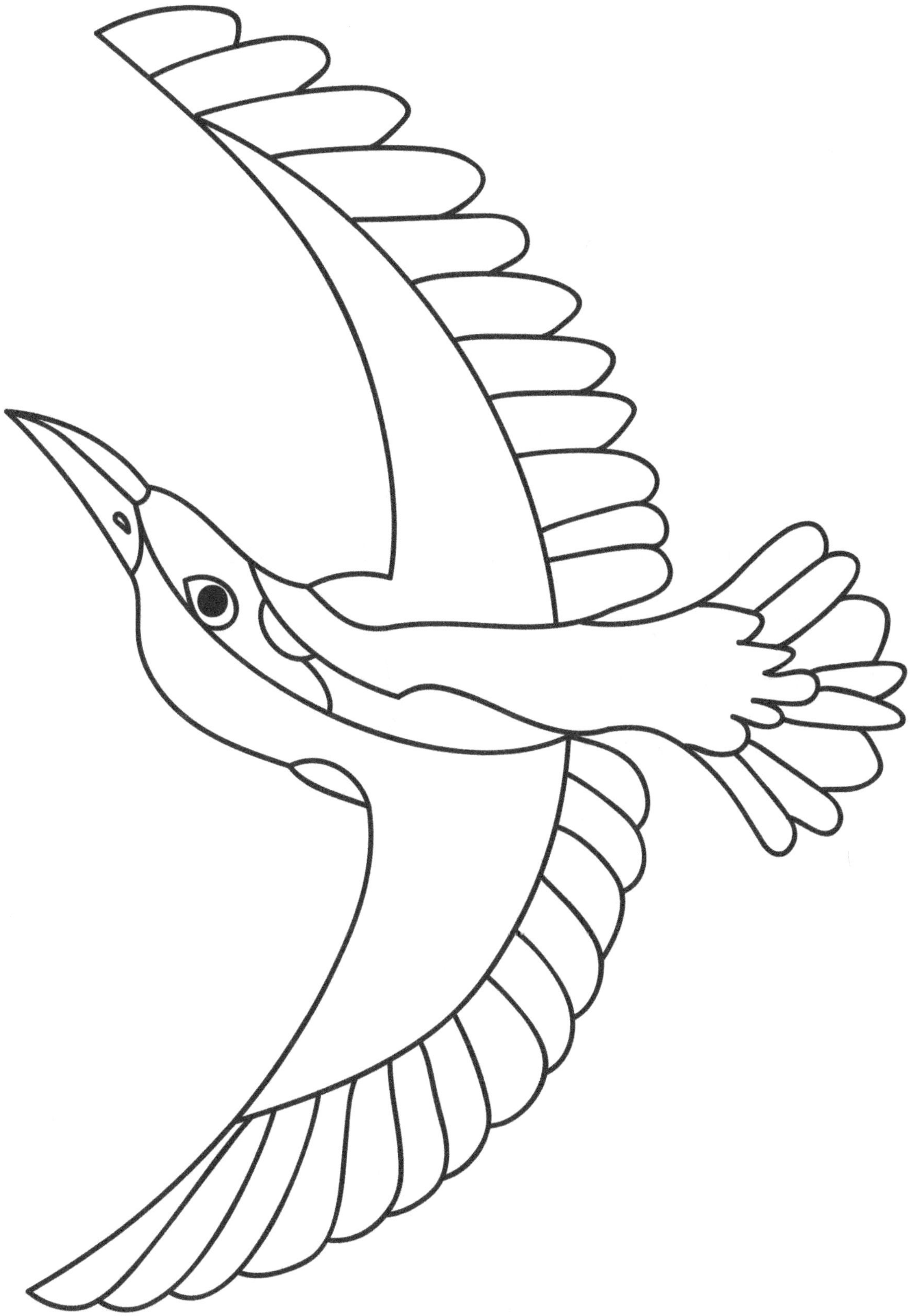

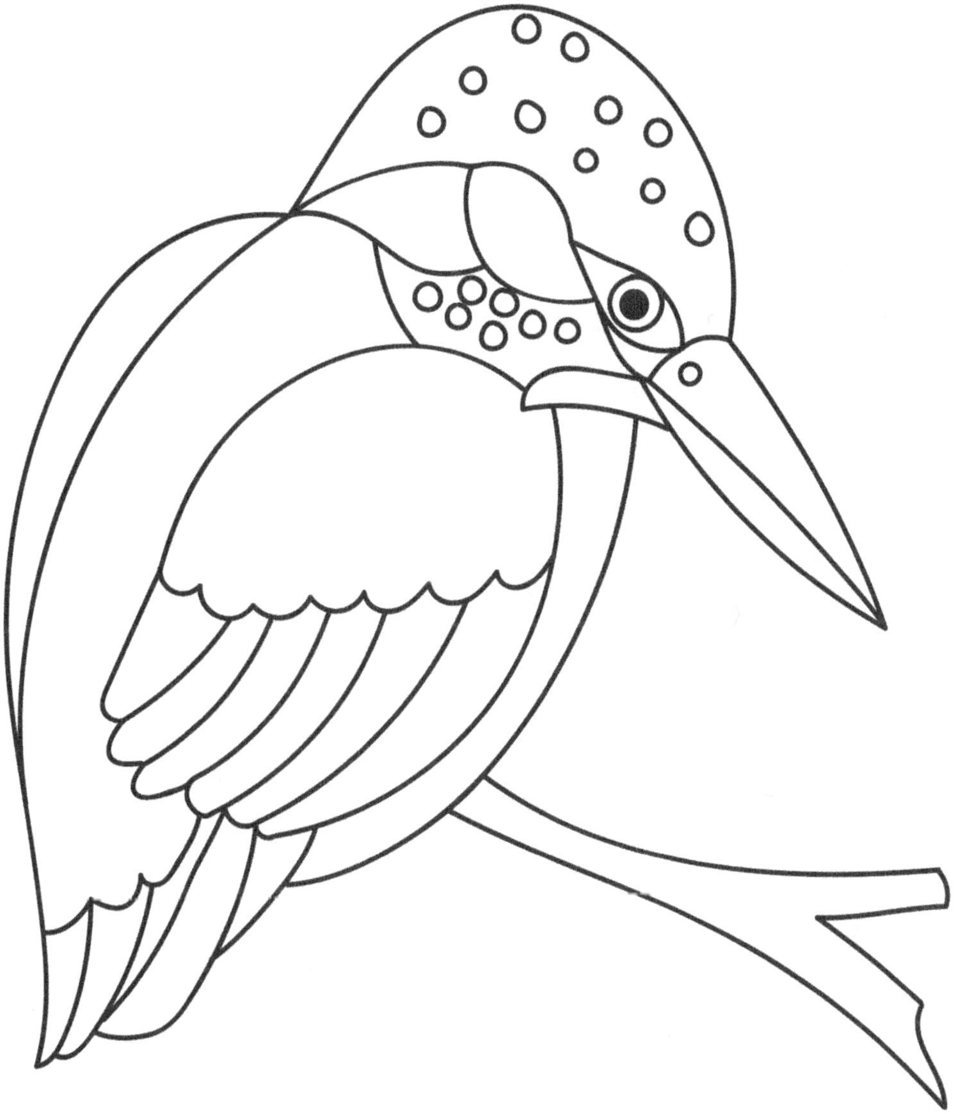

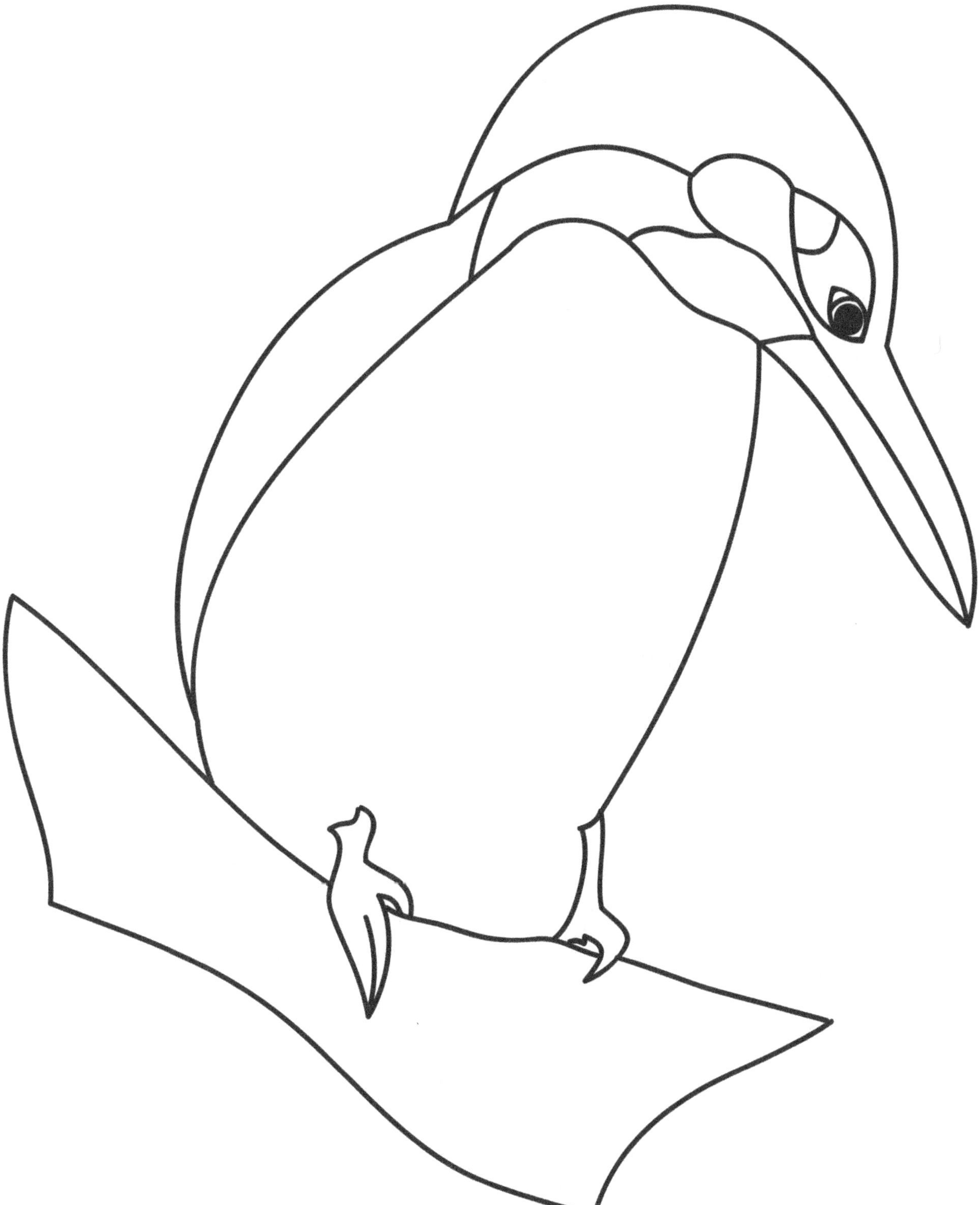

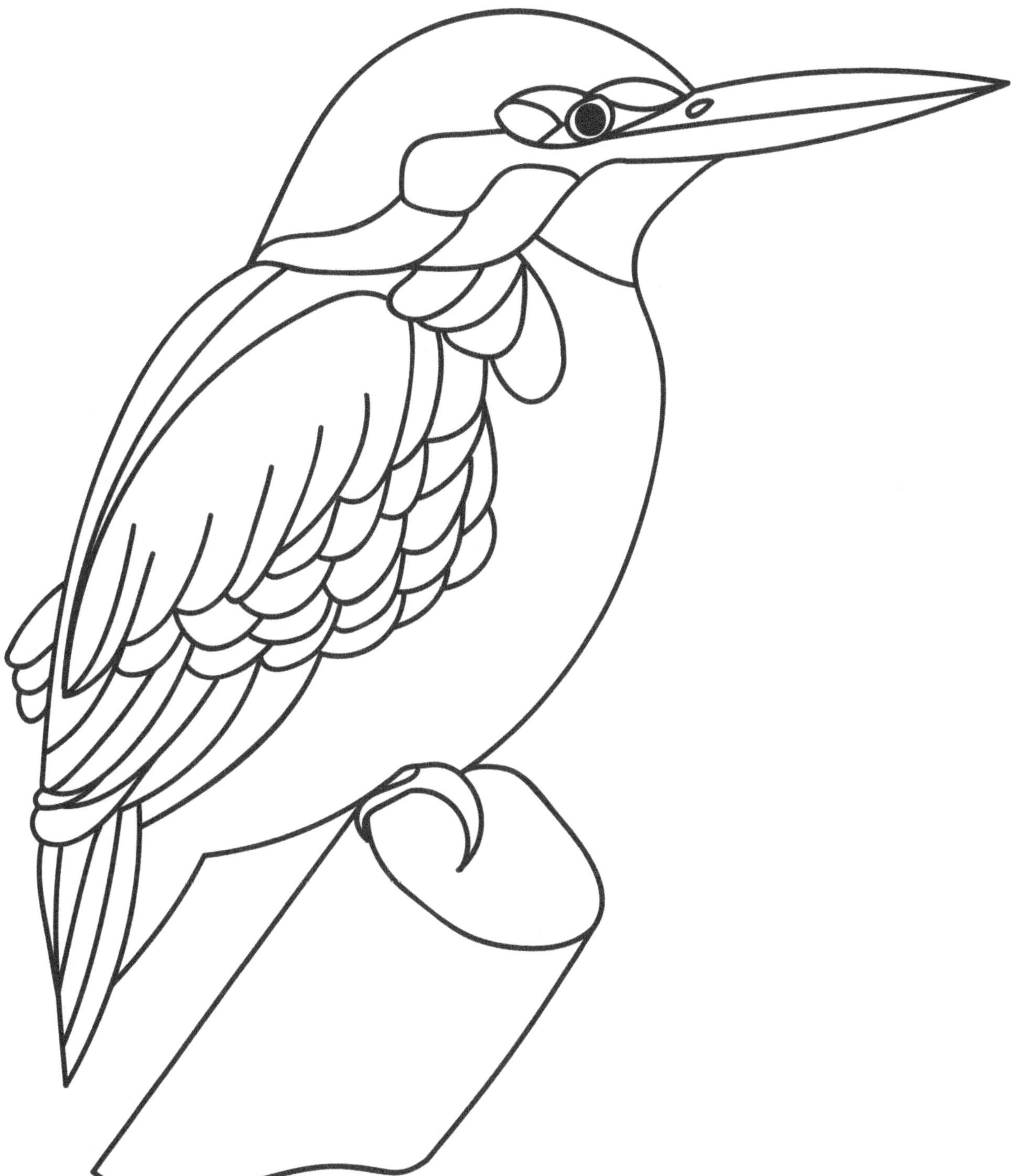

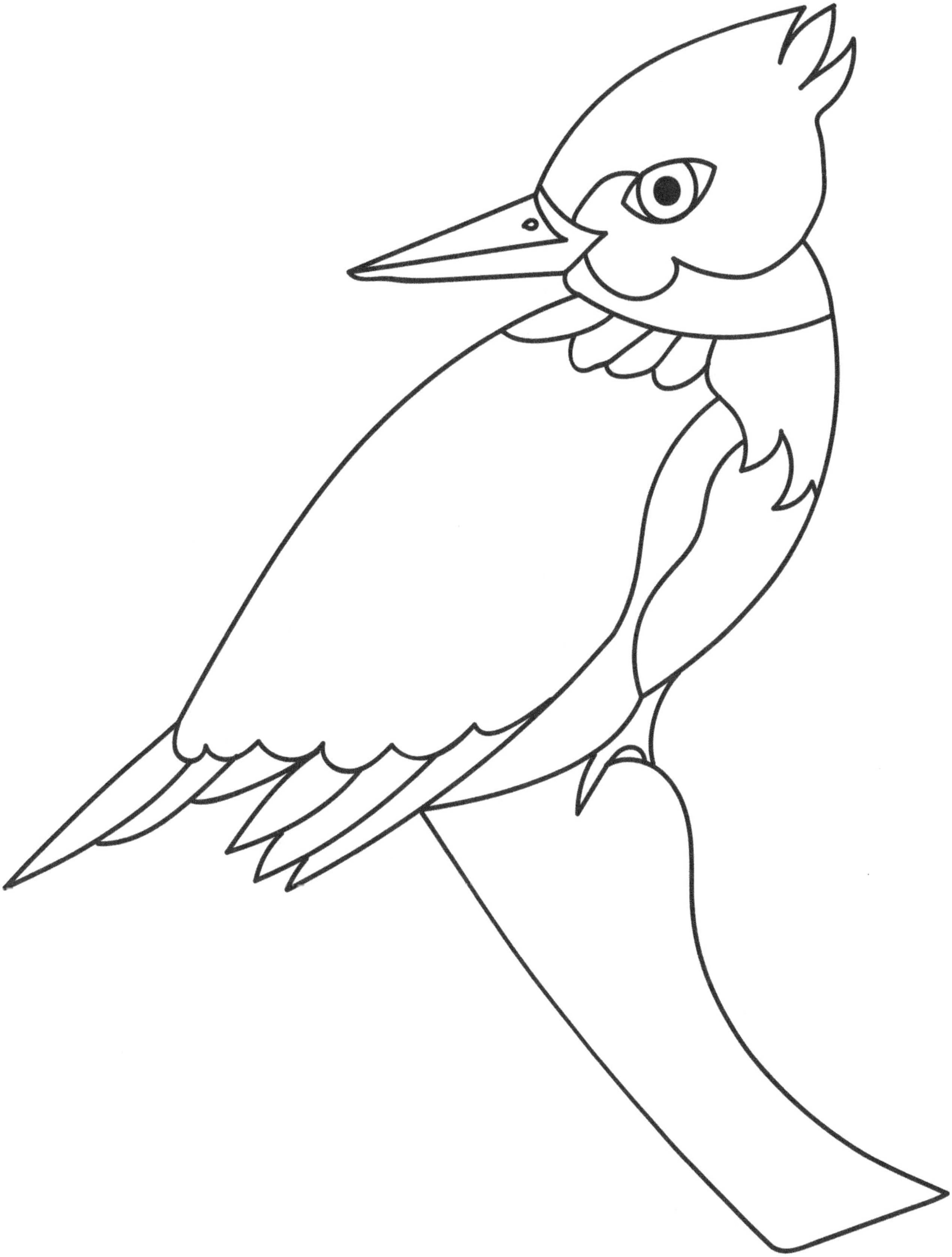

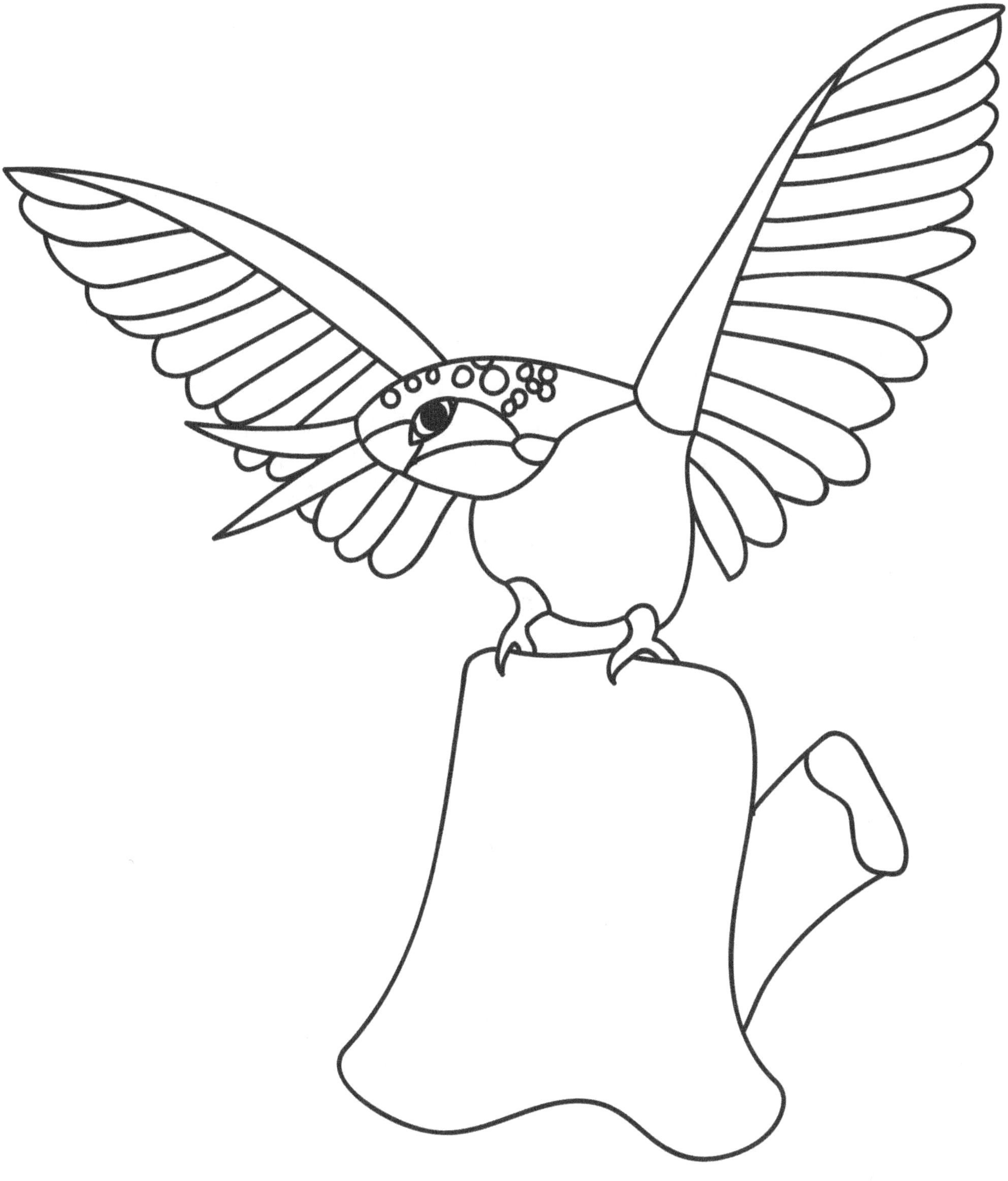

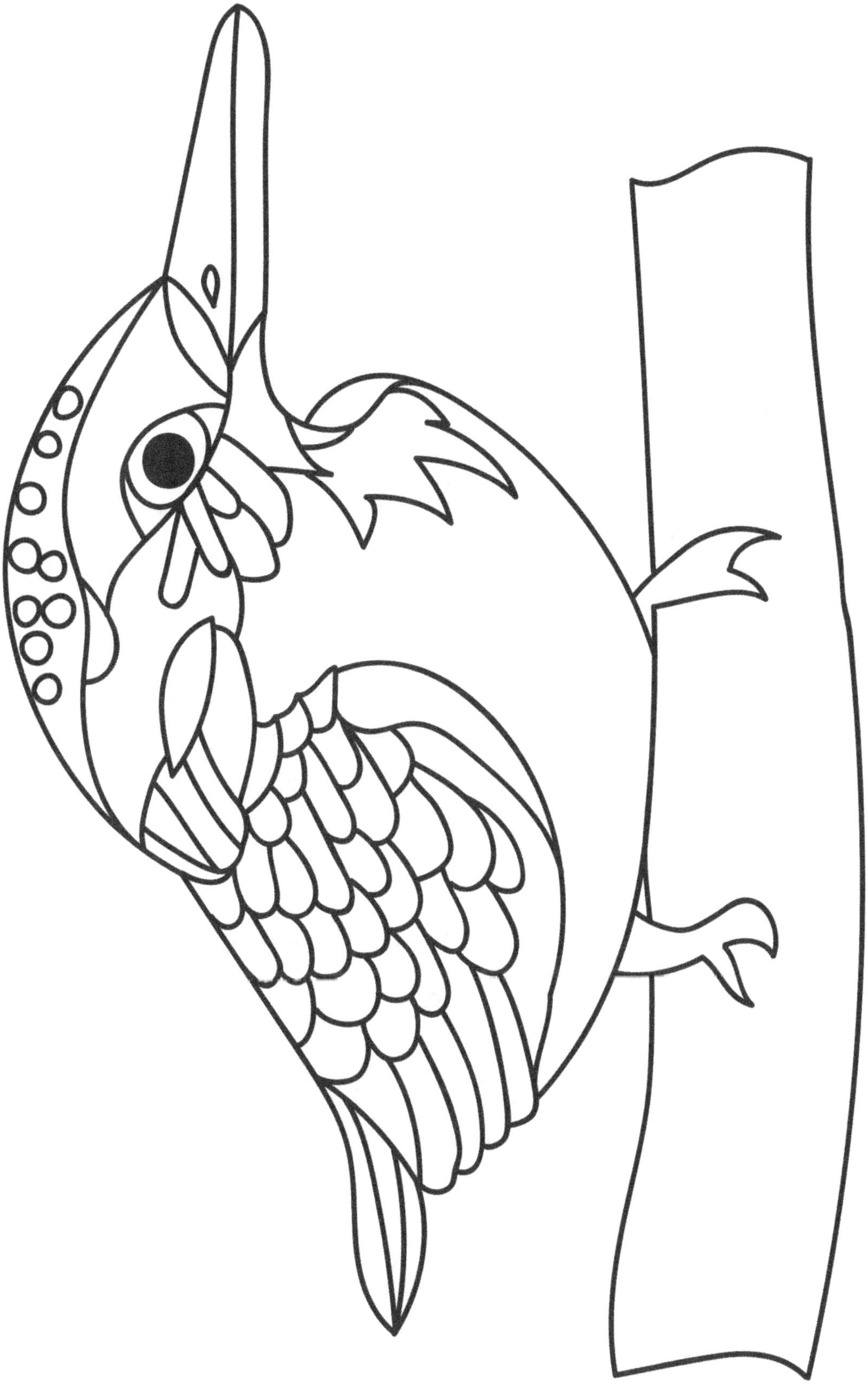

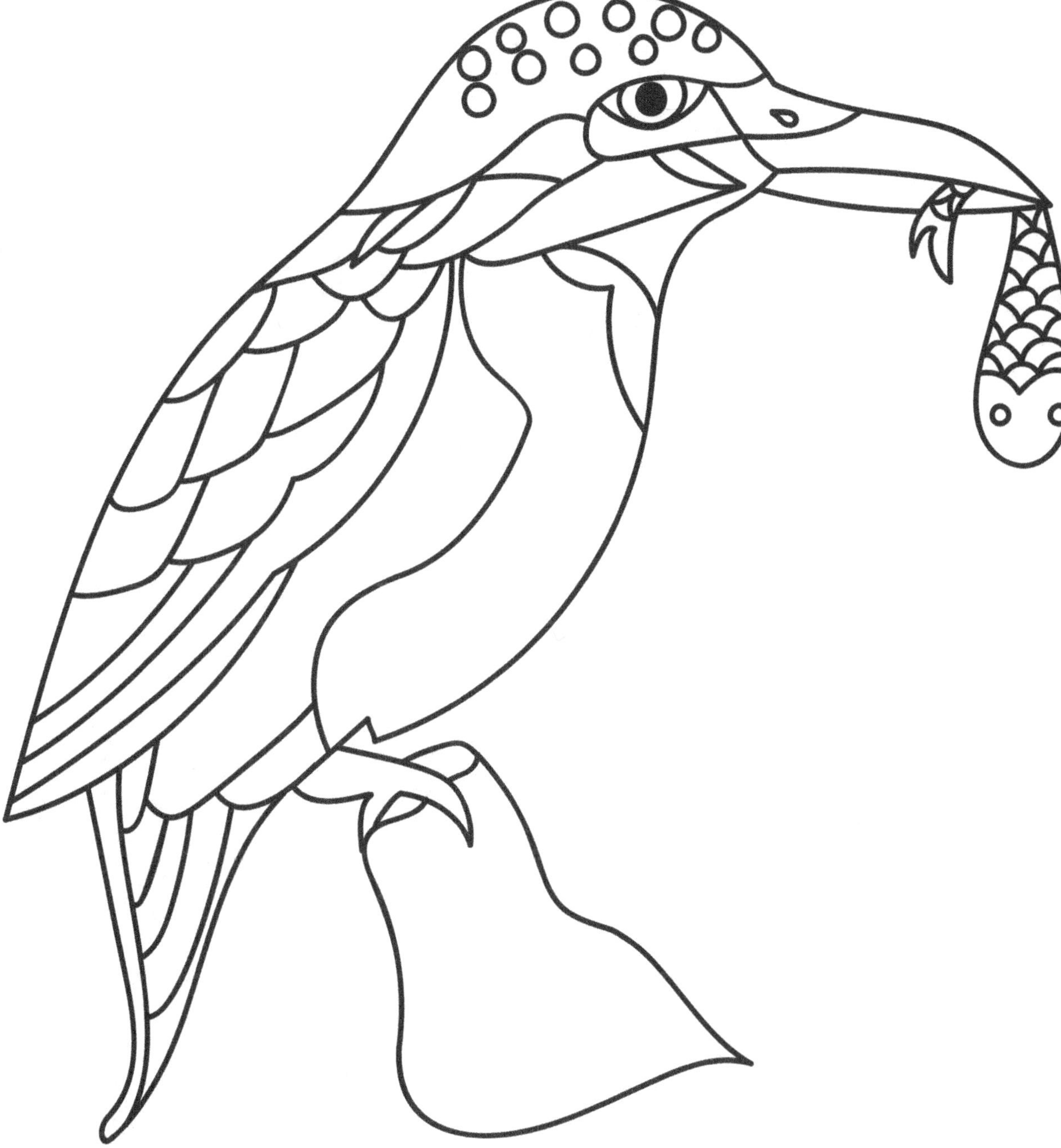

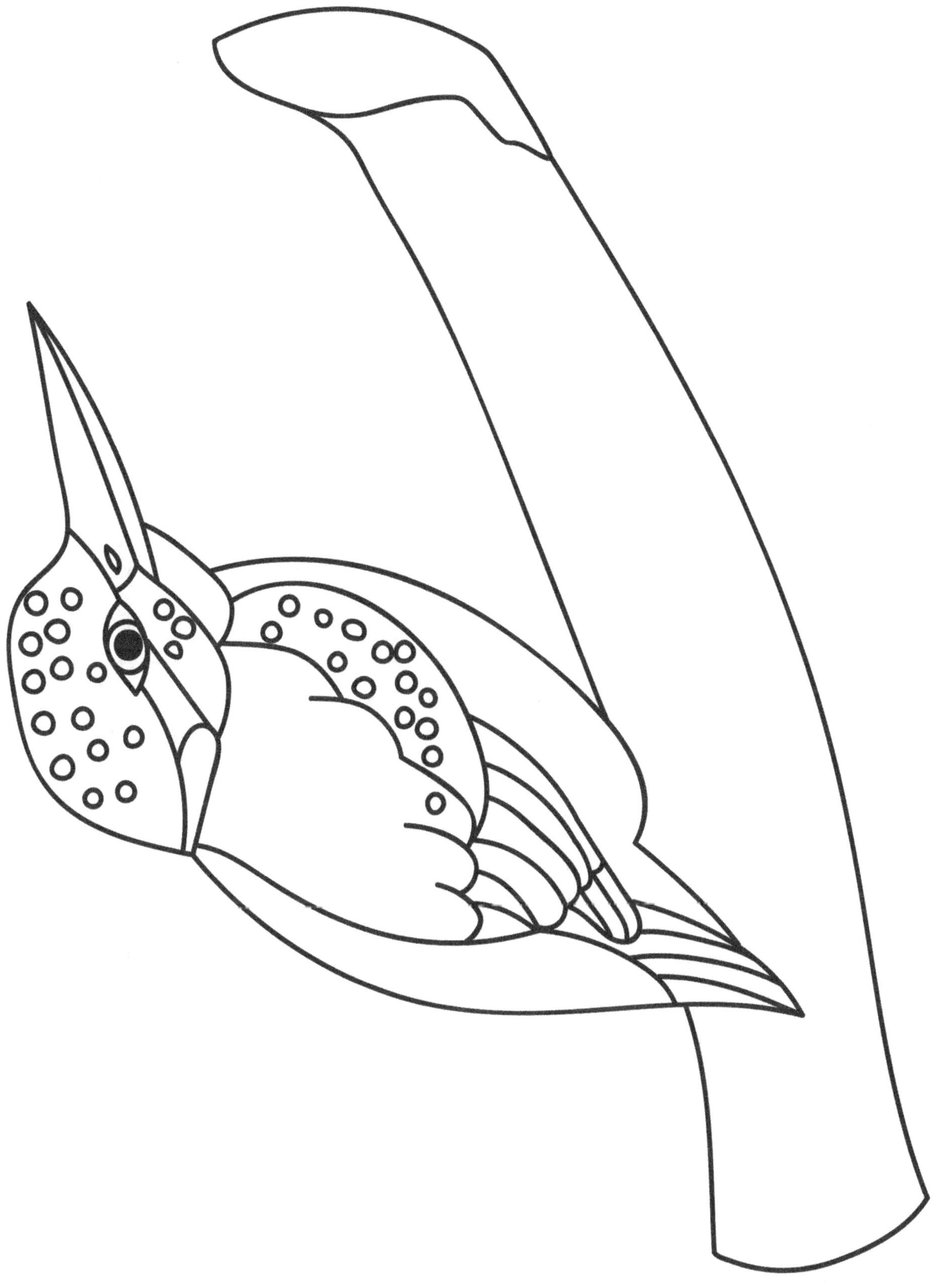

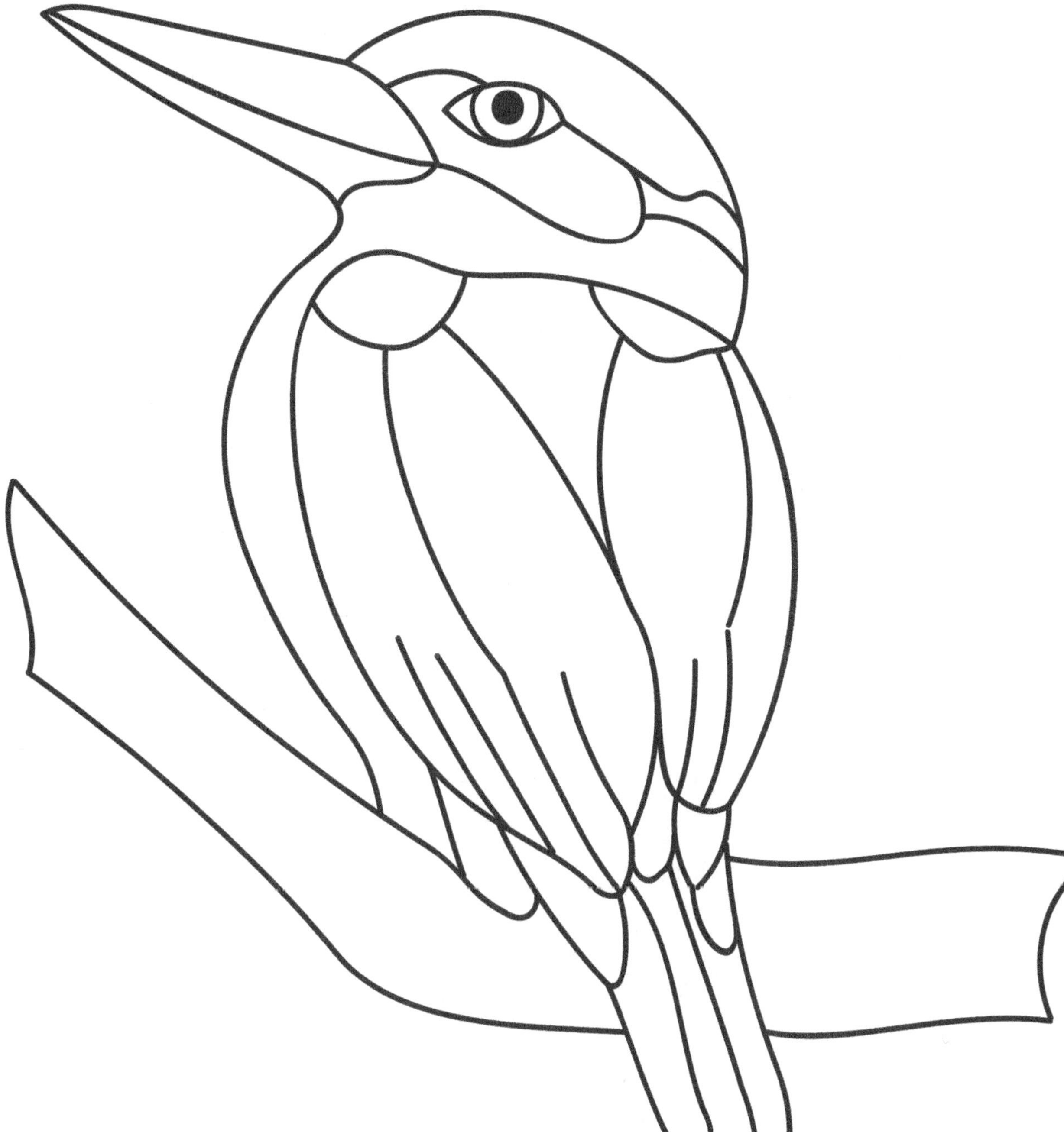

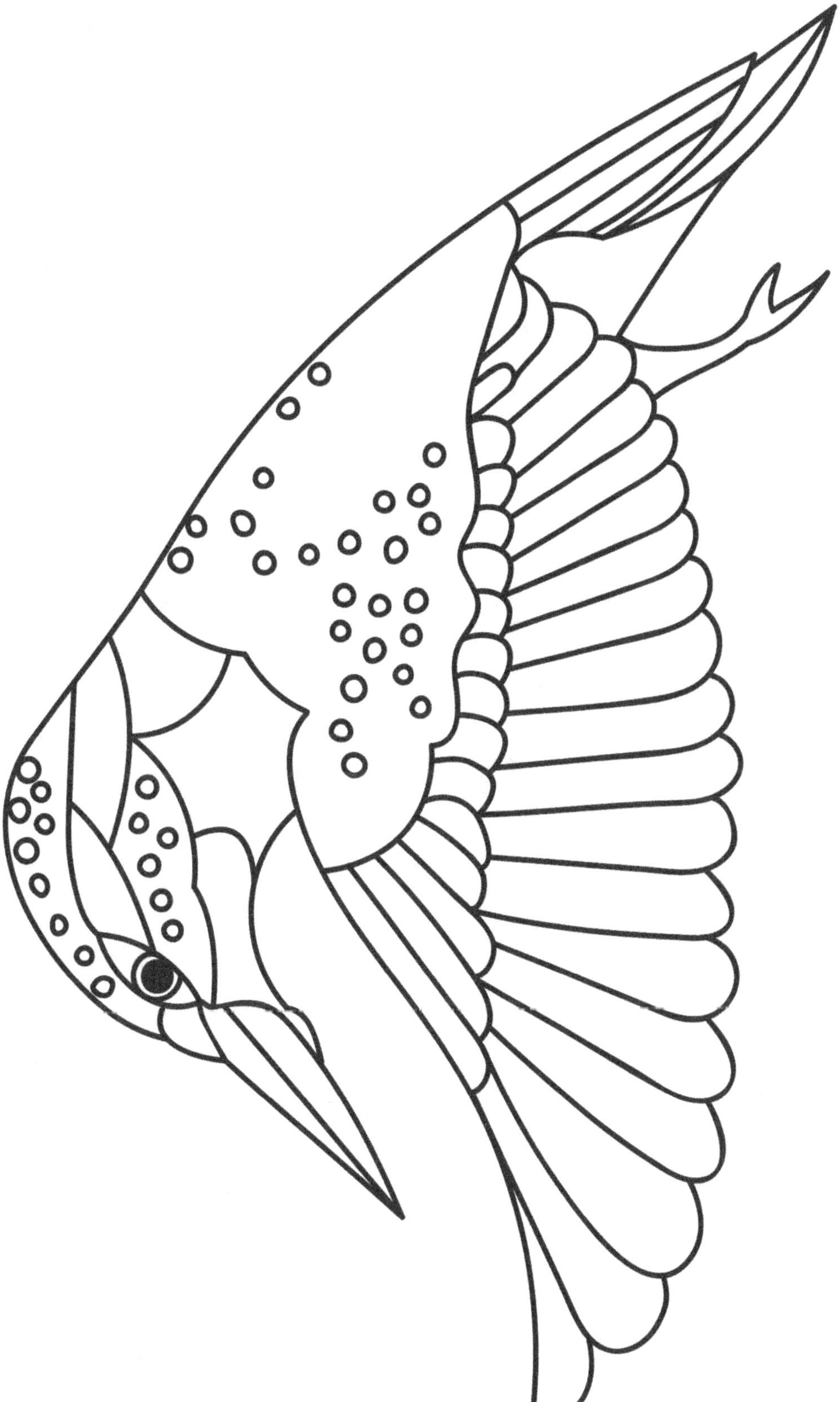

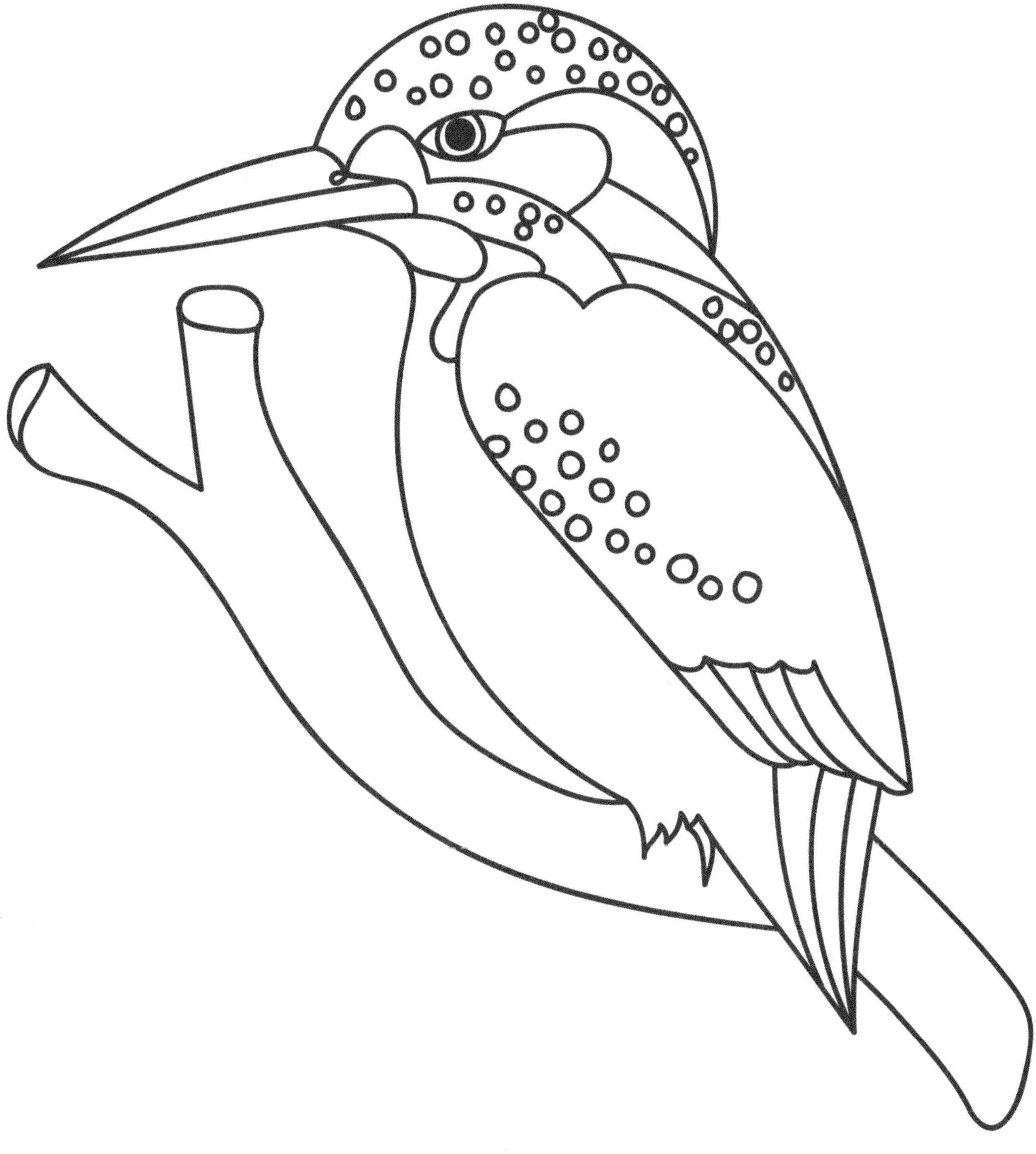

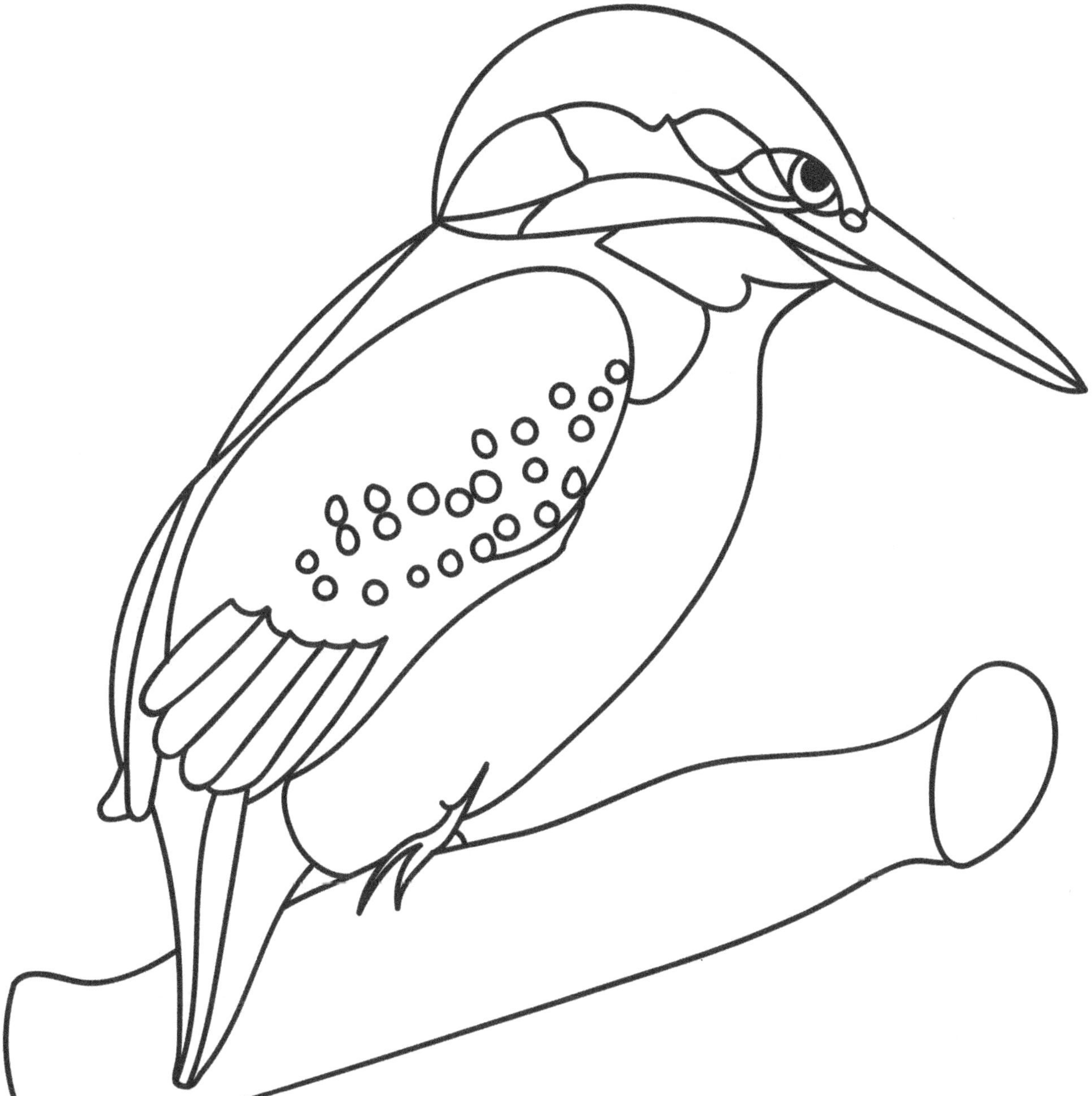

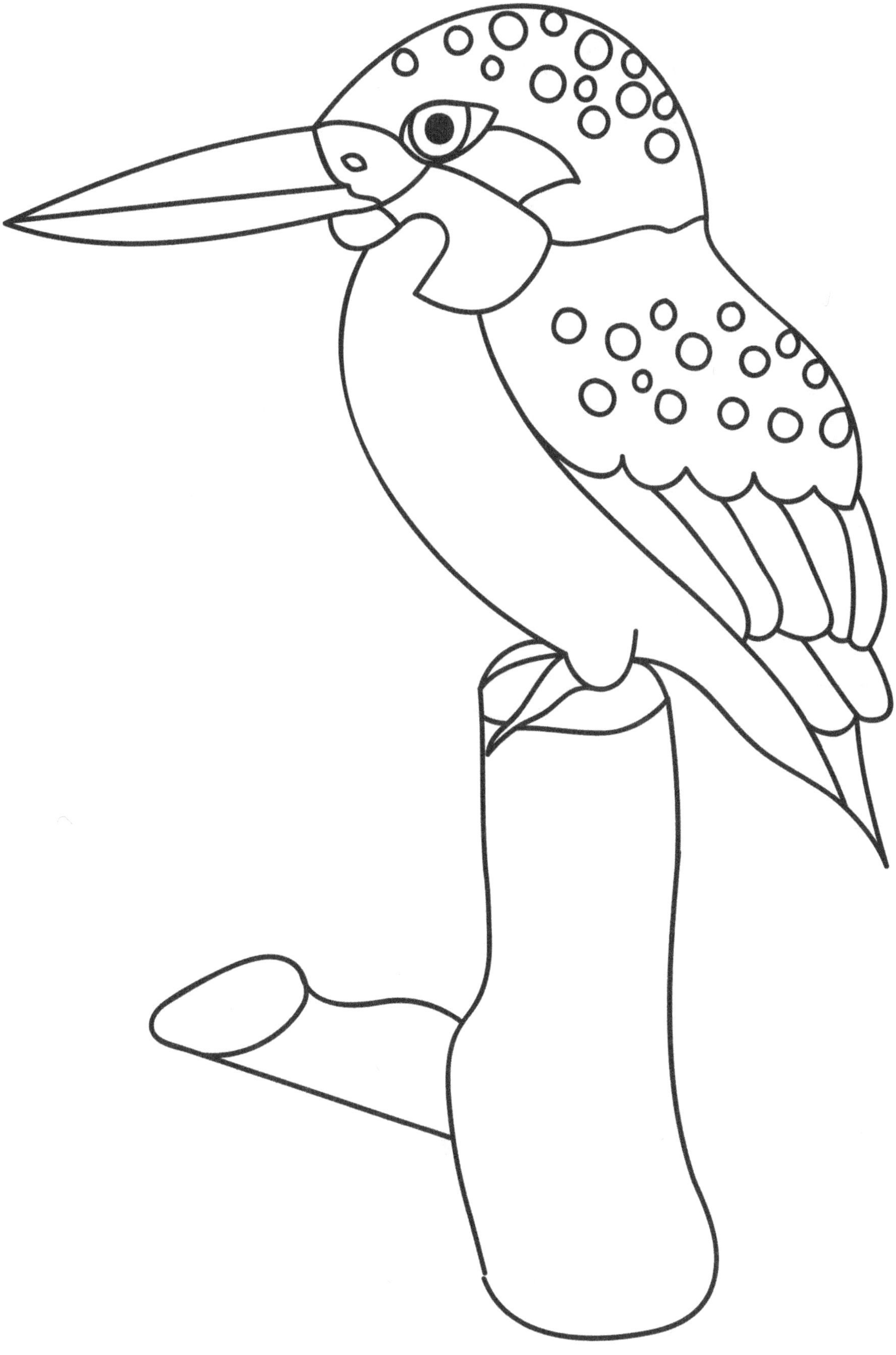

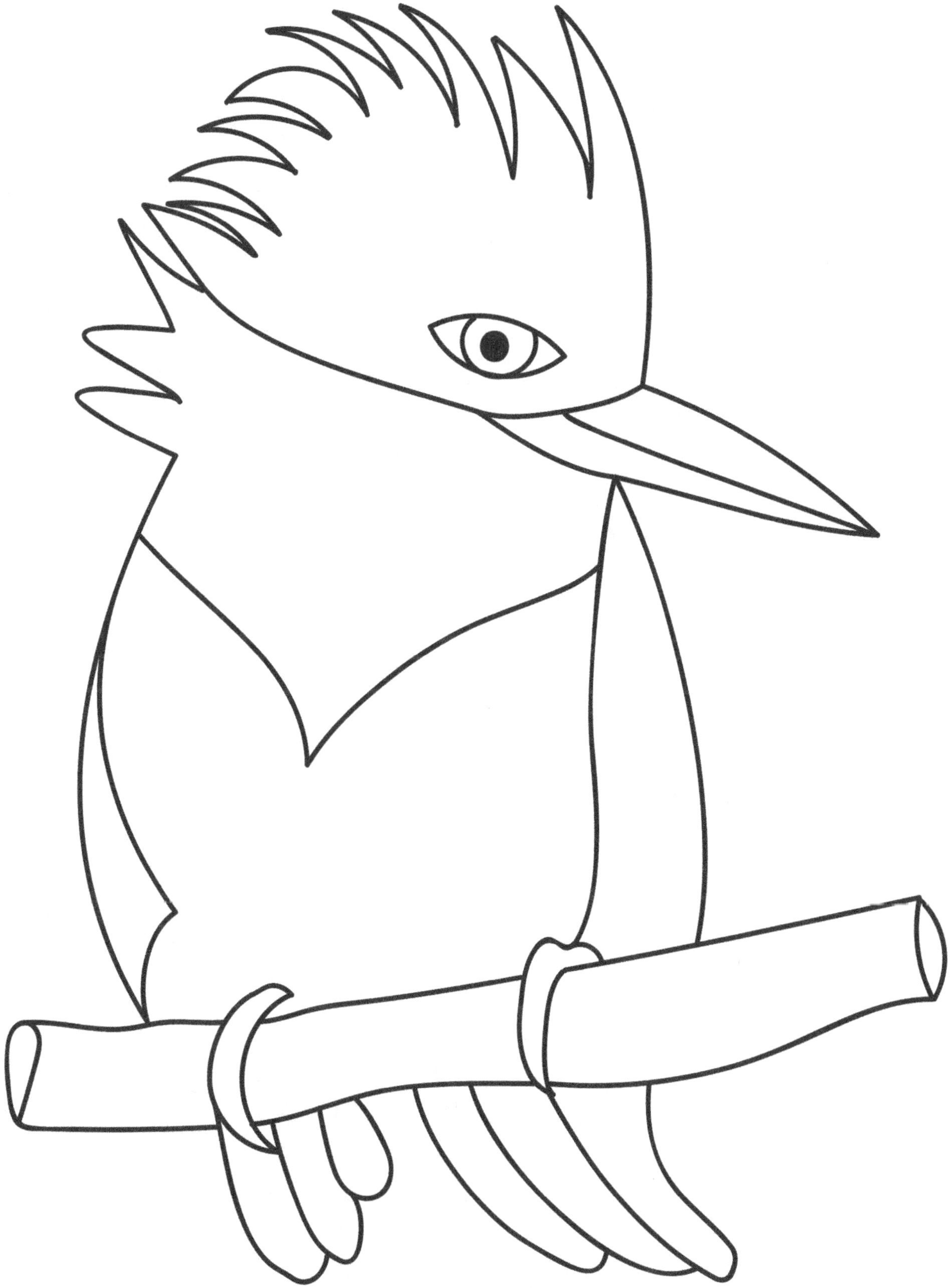

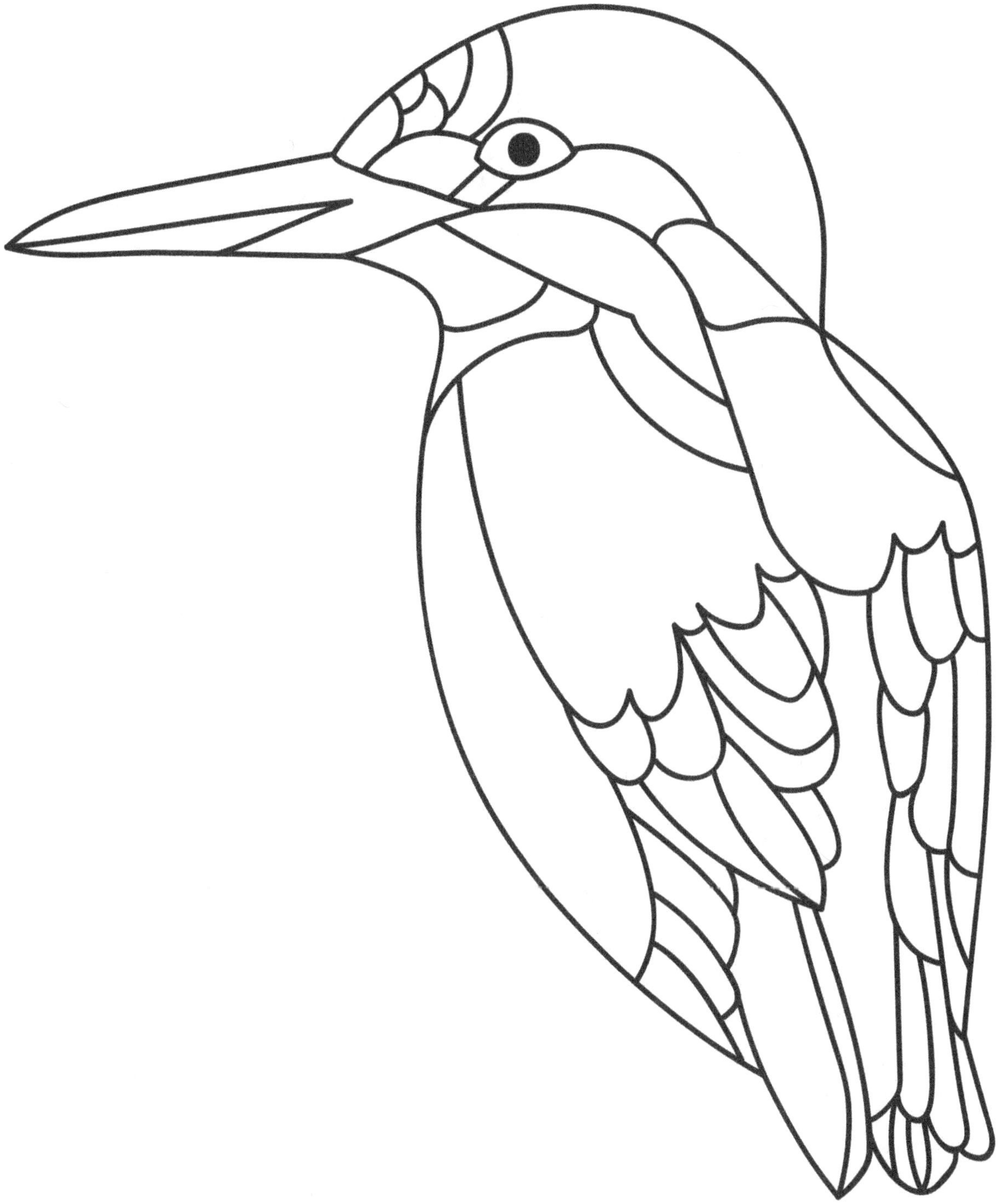

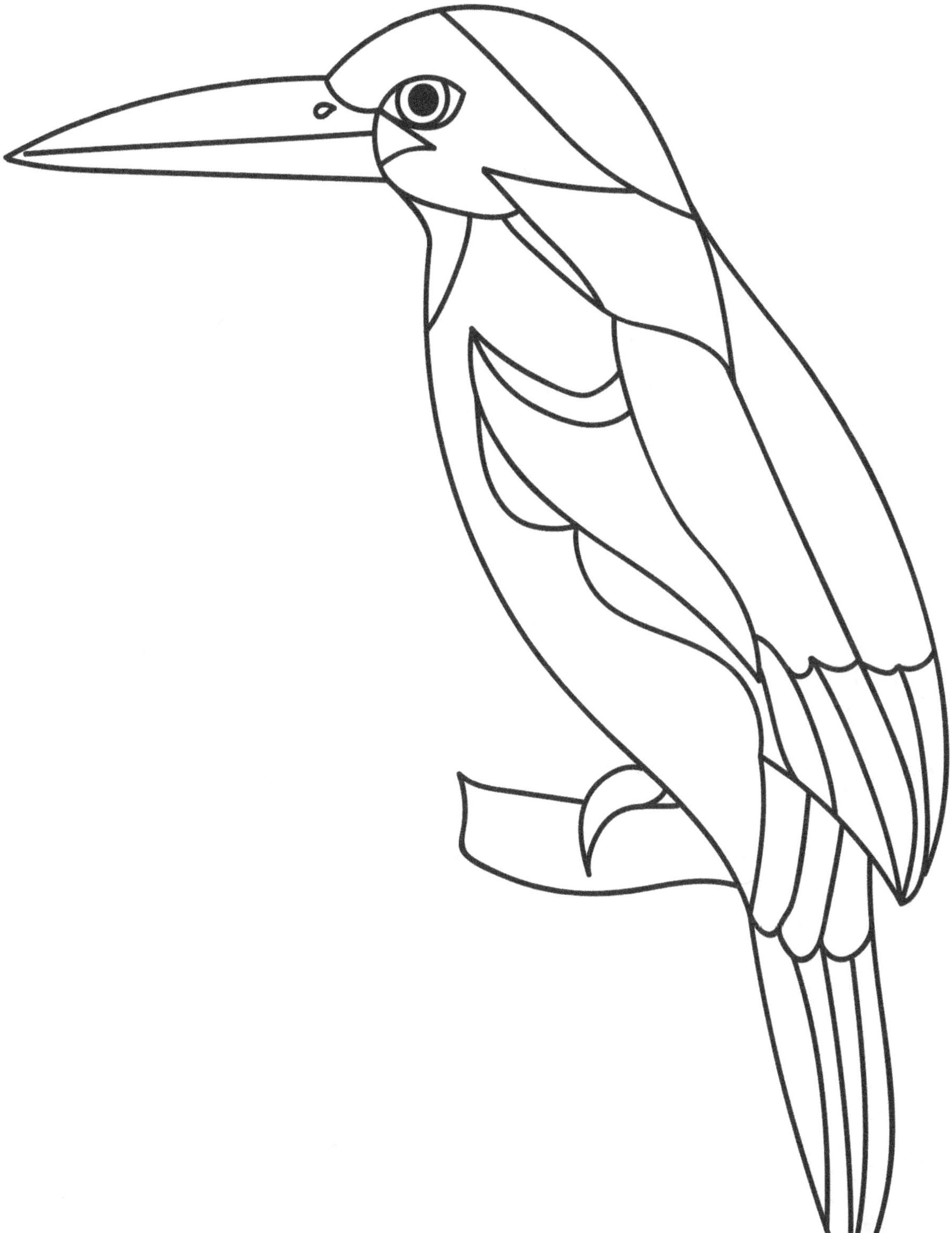

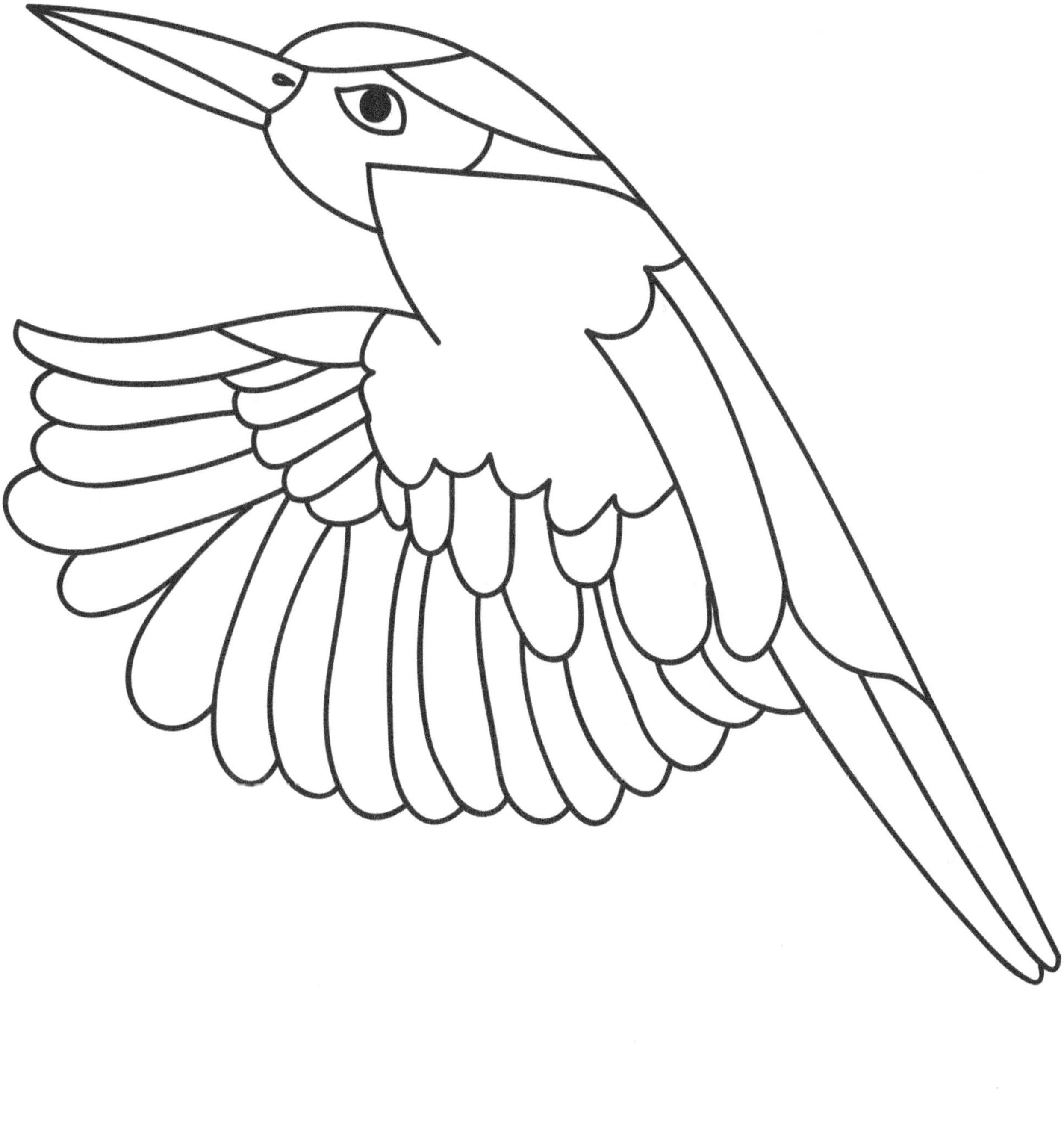

COLOR TEST PAGE

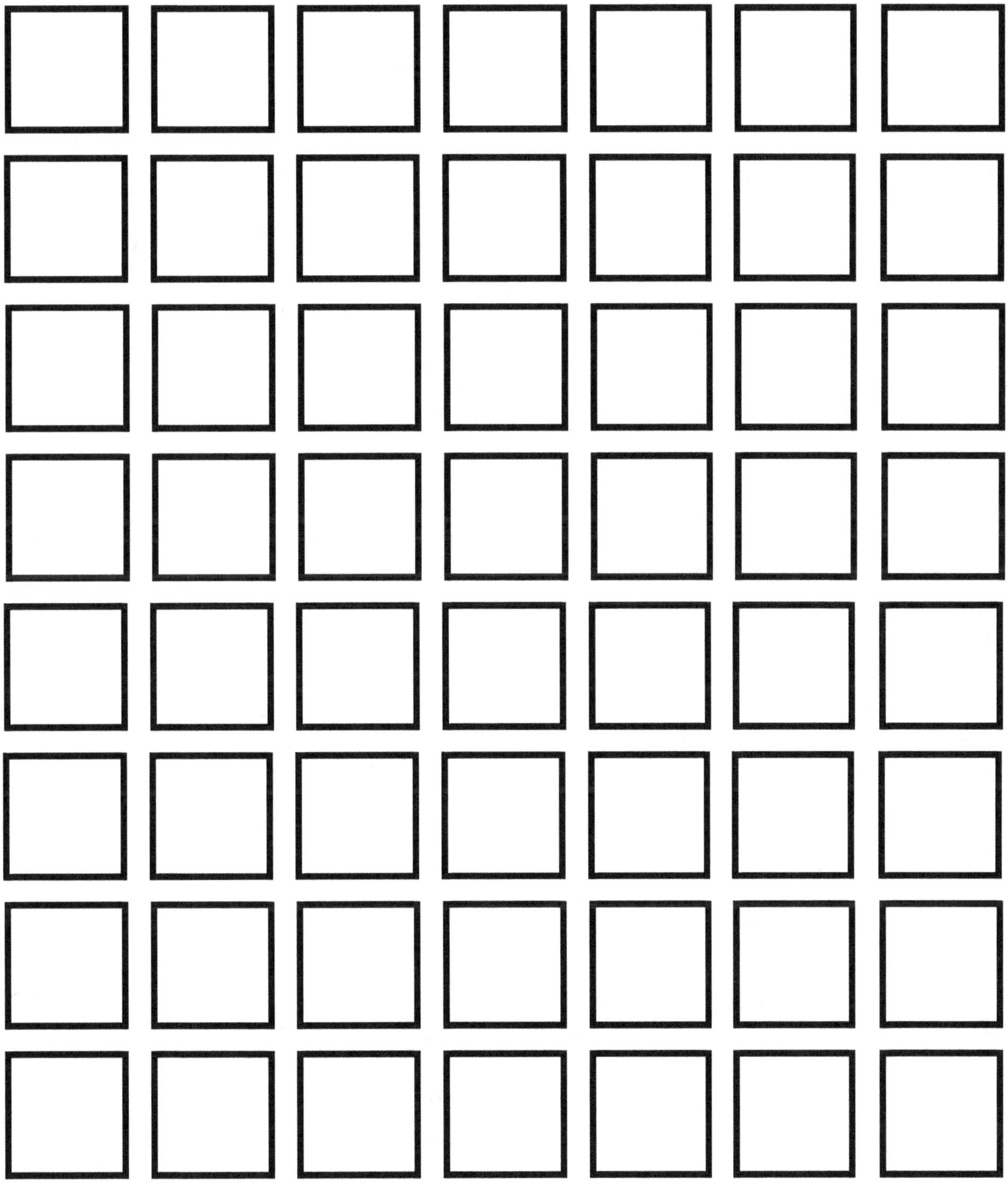

COLOR TEST PAGE

www.ingramcontent.com/pod-product-compliance
Lightning Source LLC
Chambersburg PA
CBHW062122220526
45471CB00010B/3843
* 9 7 8 1 9 8 7 4 8 5 1 2 7 *